Eagles in the Dust
Alcohol and Other Chemical Pastimes

I dedicate this book, first, to my Celestial Beloveds: the Báb, Bahá'u'lláh, 'Abdu'l-Bahá, Shoghi Effendi, the Hands of the Cause, and the Universal House of Justice. They gave my life purpose and meaning, served as Exemplar, reared the Administrative Order, shepherded humanity through a turbulent transition, and guide the Bahá'í community through the challenging process of creating a glorious new world. Without these figures and institutions, I would lack the perception, purpose and impetus to present my meagre thoughts.

I dedicate this, as well, to my earthly beloveds: my children Eli and Layli – I hope this work guides you in years to come and offers a window into my heart and mind. To my wife Jenny – you've stood by me in all my stumbles, overlooked my foolishness and faults, and smiled at my silliness. Thank you, my dear Jenna.

Finally, I offer a quotation that has inspired and guided my path for two decades, and represents the aspiration of my entire life:

> Put all your beliefs into harmony with science; there can be no opposition, for truth is one. When religion, shorn of its superstitions, traditions, and unintelligent dogmas, shows its conformity with science, then will there be a great unifying, cleansing force in the world which will sweep before it all wars, disagreements, discords and struggles – and then will mankind be united in the power of the Love of God.
>
> *'Abdu'l-Bahá*

Eagles in the Dust

Alcohol and Other Chemical Pastimes

Robert Cacchioni

GR

GEORGE RONALD • OXFORD

George Ronald, Publisher
Oxford
www.grbooks.com

A catalogue record for this book is available from the British Library

ISBN 978-0-85398-625-6

Cover design: René Steiner, Steinergraphics.com

Contents

Foreword

The Bahá'í Faith has no clergy. With this, no individual can claim an authoritative or binding interpretation of its Writings. This book, therefore, though rooted in Bahá'í scripture, represents no more than the thoughts and understanding of its author.

This work is born of decades of thought, and in some instances personal experience, on the topic of alcohol and drugs. In many ways, it is a work of passion. The author feels that the common practice of alcohol and drug use needs attention, and more so, conceptual reframing.

Some years before the formation of this work, the National Spiritual Assembly of Canada – the Canadian Bahá'í community's elected body – requested increased attention to the Bahá'í stance on alcohol and drug use, and the reasons given for it. This work – after much consultation, discussion and partial presentations – is the fruit of that request, now snowballed into a full book after these many years.

Although this work is inspired by the Bahá'í Writings, the arguments presented here are not inherently religious. I believe that whether religious, atheist or anything in between, you won't need any 'suspended belief' or 'leaps of faith' to understand or appreciate the concepts offered to you.

Bahá'u'lláh – the Prophet-Founder of the Bahá'í Faith – states:

> It is inadmissible that man, who hath been endowed with reason, should consume that which stealeth it away. Nay, rather it behoveth him to comport himself in a manner worthy of the human station . . .

This small verse contains the most simplified expression of the author's core concern, the tiny seed that birthed a tree.

Make no mistake, whether Bahá'í or not, religious or not, the author asks you to give up alcohol – not out of fear of God, not out of raw religious obligation, nor social convention. He explains why he believes mankind should have abandoned this practice long ago.

All authors, I'm quite sure, hope to reach as broad an audience as possible; this case is no exception. Alongside this considerable task, topics such as this often bring out powerful emotions, which make communication all the more difficult. Readers should, of course, have emotions, though it places an added difficulty on any author attempting to balance 'overkill' and 'subtlety' over a broad range of potential readers. Because alcohol – amongst varied other drugs – is quite deeply woven into the fabric of Western culture, this may also result in some parts feeling more jarring than others. The author, of course, does not seek to offend or upset. Yet, as with any work of the heart, there will be an intensity to sections which will be quite noticeable. Naturally, questioning deeply ingrained social practices makes choosing the appropriate level of intensity challenging, though hopefully not impossible. True balance coupled with eloquence can rarely be struck, and the author, I assure you, does not claim to have achieved this.

Some people have never personally struggled with alcohol

or other intoxicants, and these pages will be more an intellectual pursuit, one of curiosity. For others, these substances have impacted them indirectly. Yet, they themselves may have never battled with addiction, nor felt the impact in their home. They may seek to expand their understanding of these issues, to hear the 'other side'.

For some readers, drugs or alcohol has damaged their family, or harmed the lives of friends. Others will most certainly have intimately grappled with these substances. For such people, this work may have near-literally felt heavier to pick up off a table or shelf. These souls will have garnered an extra share of respect for their willingness to endure such discomfort.

Because people will inevitably approach this topic from various vantage-points, parts of this book may feel tedious or overly comprehensive, others too quickly glossed. Sections may appear lighthearted, while others too heavy, even if this has diligently sought to be avoided through repeated edits. That some sections would speak more deeply (or differently) to some than others is expected; truly, that was the whole idea.

For my own part, I grew up in a culture where alcohol was portrayed as a social lubricant at its most benign, or – far more enticingly – as a 'forbidden fruit', a not-so-secret elixir of the adult world. Both portrayals can have their own allures to a juvenile mind. Simply and genuinely put – I wish I'd viewed my reality, my own self, and alcohol in particular in the light of how it is here portrayed. Seeing how widespread alcohol and drug use are, and highly aware of peer pressure's potential intensity, please, dear reader, contemplate how far-reaching your actions and behaviours can be on those who surround you, and watch that you are not too quick to brush off what you *expect* to be put forward in these pages.

If at the end, you understand the points presented yet still think them too heavy-handed or off the mark, you genuinely still have my admiration for trusting the author with your time. No matter what your sentiments are when you finish this work, all readers – without exception – will be presented with an option; everyone in your life will either know one more person who consumes alcohol, or one less person who does; either way, you will change your world.

Even if, at the end, you feel you are given no reason to abstain, I hope you will see those who choose otherwise in a new light – better still, a warmer light.

My thanks to you for caring enough to pick up this book,

Matthew C. Murdoch

Acknowledgements

I wish to thank those who supported and contributed to this work. First and foremost, I offer gratitude to my spiritual brother, Matthew Murdoch, who spent untold hours reviewing it, offering guidance and valuable insight. I thank him, furthermore, for his far-reaching patience with my ramblings. As well, I thank my beloved wife Jenny and my children, Eli and Layli, who sacrificed that I might offer this book. I also acknowledge the contributions of Shahrooz Shadbakht, another spiritual brother, whose useful guidance on structure and rhetoric helped me frame this work.

In addition, I must thank my foremost Bahá'í teachers. First, Jamen Zacharias, who appears in the pages of this book. His patience, willingness to sacrifice his time, and deep care for humanity enabled me to inhale the fragrance of Bahá'u'lláh's Faith. As well, Farshid Kazemi, who sacrificed many a night to patiently listen to, and then respond to my many concerns and objections. I also thank Marc Forward, who many times would forgo sleep to patiently discuss matters of great import until the sun rose.

Finally, I thank the Bahá'ís of the world, whether serving as administrators, teachers, facilitators, junior youth animators, children's class teachers – in whatever capacity – who despite the lure of comfort and temporal pleasures, sacrifice for the regeneration of the planet. You give humanity your tired moments and struggle to implement the wondrous vision of the Ancient Beauty, Bahá'u'lláh.

With deepest love, appreciation and admiration,
Robert Cacchioni

1

Packing Our Bags

The veil of normalcy

I was not born a Bahá'í. I didn't hear of Bahá'u'lláh until my mid-20s. Then, it took much reading, long debates, and a fierce internal struggle to finally accept His Revelation. It took me even longer to quit alcohol and drugs.

I knew I must abandon old patterns. Sadly, I clung to them. Alcohol and drugs had been engrained since childhood. Thus, after accepting Bahá'u'lláh, another struggle ensued. It was not easy to shake addiction's grip on my life. I embodied a condition to which Shoghi Effendi, the Guardian of the Bahá'í Faith, eloquently called attention:

> There is a difference between character and faith; it is often very hard to accept this fact and put up with it, but the fact remains that a person may believe in and love the Cause – even to being ready to die for it – and yet not have a good personal character, or possess traits at variance with the teachings. We should try to change, to let the Power of God help recreate us and make us true Bahá'ís in deed as well as in belief. But sometimes the process is slow, sometimes it never happens because the individual does not try hard enough.

But these things cause us suffering and are a test to us in our fellow-believers, most especially if we love them and have been their teacher![1]

I believed in Bahá'u'lláh, wanted to dedicate my life to His Cause, but had – in *many* respects – a poor character. Though not an excuse, drinking alcohol was customary in my world – that of an everyday Canadian – an expected part of life. I grew up surrounded by alcohol. With a 'healthy dose' of rebellion, I'd sneak a sip, can or bottle at family functions prior to high school – often with a wink or a half-smile from an adult.

Once I had grown up (at the ripe old age of 13), I consumed large amounts weekly. From teens to 25, I drank every week, and always in ample amounts. I started smoking pot in the first year of high school.

At social gatherings, I expected an exciting guest list – beer, hard liquor, and various other substances – some more hidden than others, some more dangerous. Alcohol flowed along with life's natural rhythms. If sad, we drank. Happy? We drank. Celebrating? We drank. At weddings, funerals, vacations, birthdays – or honestly, any weekend – we drank. The hidden substances – eventually ranging from marijuana, to LSD, on up to cocaine – were *recreational* drugs, a way to have fun. Honestly, I never questioned this 'natural order'. Why would I?

An unquestioning acceptance of mind-altering substances should not surprise anyone; every restaurant serves liquor; coworkers delight in stories of weekend chemical excursions; movies, commercials, and television portray alcohol as a desirable diversion. Liquor's uplifting effects are lauded in song and theatre daily. In our day, marijuana is both extolled and pervasive. Chemical pastimes surround us more and more.

Inundated by a recreational-chemical culture, maybe a clear perspective eludes us. Pub propaganda and club culture dominates the social arena. In such circumstances, we often can't consider another course. Normalcy numbs us to alternate paths. It always does.

Constant exposure can make anything miraculous seem mundane. Imagine standing in the Louvre in Paris. One of Da Vinci's most revered works – the Mona Lisa – hangs before you, an object admired for centuries, a recognized masterpiece. You stand in awe, stunned by the precision, acutely aware of Leonardo's prowess. Your heart floods with admiration, tinged with envy. As you leave the Louvre, by some miracle, the curators gift you the painting. You now own the Mona Lisa. Da Vinci's work of genius will adorn your living room wall.

At first, you immerse yourself in Leonardo's expertise. Friends, family and acquaintances beg to join you. You bathe in its beauty, experiencing the awe you felt in the Louvre, mesmerized by her entrancing smile. Daily, you discover intricacies previously unseen. For a long while, you delight in the envy of family, friends and acquaintances. Then slowly, imperceptibly so, things change.

Months roll by, and a transformation begins. You admire it occasionally. Once in a while, you stop to appreciate its exquisiteness, for a moment carried back to that first time in Paris, a time now receding into the mists of memory.

Much later, however, you pass it – without a glance – on your way to the bathroom. As you watch a boring movie, it hangs behind you, unnoticed. You cart in your groceries after a long day without even a peep. A day comes when you sit reading in your chair, and the Mona Lisa's priceless visage peers ineffectually over your shoulder from its now-lonely place on the wall.

This transformation is typical. What we once found miraculous or glorious slides into the category of the mundane, the ordinary. It is often imperceptible, until the damage is done. Yet we all know the danger.

People hitherto passionately in love take each other for granted. Former devoted lovers pay only passing attention to the *one* they promised their life to. This is why death wrenches us from the grip of the mundane; we're suddenly slammed with the degree to which the deceased enriched our lives. This numbing path to normalcy allows precious moments with our children to pass into oblivion. Potential moments of wonder slide behind a drab and foggy veil – the veil of normalcy.

Predictably, the veil of normalcy works in the opposite way. If your living room housed manure instead of the Mona Lisa, you'd become accustomed to the odour, dimly aware of its aroma, if at all. Objects of intense beauty or disgust – Mona Lisa or manure – can become mundane.

With repeated exposure, shocking, frightening, or downright disgusting experiences become routine. Life in a war zone would cripple me psychologically. For others, it's just another day. People go about their business as missiles carve the sky and shots ring out in the streets. Starvation, disease and abject poverty damaged my mind when I lived in Yemen – at first. To me, the sight of shanty towns, squalor and disease caused shock. For the local inhabitants, that's life – business as usual – and these sights become the backdrop, a hum filtered out by long acquaintance.

In past ages, traders *naturally* sold humans at the marketplace. Blood flooded the Roman Colosseum year after year. Now however, we might vomit, shudder or begin screaming at either practice. For many, it was routine; for some, entertainment. Why question what has been there all along? That's just the way it is. And hey, don't knock it 'til ya try it. The norm it was – but not the way it was meant to be, I think you'll agree.

And maybe, alcohol and drug use appear normal for the same reason.

Remember the veil of normalcy on our coming expedition.

You may well at certain times think me extreme in analogy or metaphor. You might think, 'Come on. It's not *that* bad!' If this happens, please pause and consider this possibility – the veil of normalcy obscures your perspective, so naturally I appear severe. Yet maybe drugs and alcohol would seem indefensible to those who felt no attachment to them.

Hence, I predict that many people will view my position as excessive. Currently, everyone effortlessly understands the depravity of Roman gladiatorial games – doing so in 200 AD would have been far more difficult. In certain circles, you'd have been taken for a killjoy – even if it was a human death-sport. Many believed Martin Luther King Jr. was excessive in demanding *immediate* equality in the Civil Rights Movement. At the end of the 18th century, 'radical' applied to advocates of universal male suffrage – note the 'male' in that phrase.

These understandings now appear easy to all. Yet, if you understand what I am saying, questioning alcohol will likely be challenging. Because of pub propaganda and club culture, it all seems so 'normal'. Thus, it is no surprise that individuals see abstainers as oddities, or even as puritans and prudes – fanatically fleeing from fun. Some even see abstinence as a character defect.

In spite of the cultural momentum against me, I have hope. I believe in humanity, and, therefore, believe we can tear away such veils; we have before. And if on our journey, I cannot tear it away, I hope I can, at least, lift a corner of the veil.

Beginning the temple tour

Today, we begin a journey, touring four *temples*, each dedicated to an aspect of humankind. We will visit the temples of *body*, *heart*, *mind* and *soul*. On this tour, you have a guide: me. Naturally, I will express my feelings, share thoughts, and call attention to each temple's worth – and I hope you will agree.

At each stop, we'll reflect on the temple's beauty and contrast its grandeur with our culture's *recreational* use of chemicals: alcohol and drugs.

To be frank, I want everyone – for love of self and others – to renounce these substances and live a more pure and progressive life. I cannot (and would not want to) hide this. I believe these chemicals harm humanity, stunt our growth and impede cultural progress – as abrupt as that may sound. I don't want to sound technical or clinical, and so I will express sorrow at the damage I believe alcohol and drugs cause.

I believe that if we cast aside our attachments to drugs and alcohol, humankind would find new reservoirs of inner joy and peace. We would explore new and natural avenues of human growth. We would begin to flourish. Therefore, love for humanity and passion for our potential gave birth to this book.

Further, I do not merely hope people stop *using* these chemicals; I long for (and work for) a world that does not *desire* them. Finally, I hope that if we do not agree, you will, at least, understand (by the end) why I think as I do.

As with any journey, we must pack our bags before setting off. Because our journey is intellectual, we need concepts, not clothes or credit cards. We've already packed the *numbing normalcy* idea, and have a few more things to gather before we depart.

An uncomplicated concept

Though this work is long, I don't find sobriety an odd option, nor believe the justification, in essence, to be complicated.

In my youth, I drank alcohol and used drugs. Understandably then, it stunned my friends when I suddenly stopped. One day, while visiting my hometown, my friend Dale instinctively (and courteously I might add) offered me a beer. I thanked him, politely turned it down, and suggested he enjoy himself. He looked perplexed, 'I heard you quit drinking, Rob.' I replied, 'Yes, I did,' and prepared for a debate. Then Dale asked, 'Why? I never would have expected it.' Given my past, he had good reason not to.

Longing for candour and tired of defending myself, I dropped my regular elongated rationale and asked a simple question,

'Dale, do you think the world would be a better place if people didn't use drugs and alcohol, if these substances disappeared?'

He paused for a second, 'Yeah, I'd have to agree with that.' Then, before he could suggest the assumed impossibility of such a world, I added, 'Well, then someone has to start doing it.' Dale nodded, 'Good for you Rob!' and walked to the kitchen to grab a beer.

Put simply, I believe anyone, unfettered by habit or the veil of normalcy, can recognize that the world would be healthier, more harmonious, and wiser without these substances. Nonetheless, we will take the scenic route.

What I don't do

This book's emotional tone and length misrepresent how I behave in everyday life. I don't walk around admonishing people for alcohol and drug use. I do not command people to put down the drink. I do not preach to friends and acquaintances about the ignoble effects of drugs. I don't interrupt friends' stories of their weekend excursions.

I especially refrain from discussing it when people are actively under their influence. That would be pure folly. The desire to justify their use, as well as the lowered capacity for critical thought, makes contention more likely, and conflict is not my wish.

Yet, given how rare it is to encounter an abstainer, the question invariably arises: why don't you drink? If questioned, I ask if they genuinely want an answer, rather than it being an instinctual reaction to my atypical life choice. More than once, the reply has been: 'No. Not really.' If so, I leave it alone. If they do want an answer, I offer my thoughts and feelings.

My primary goal is not (and never has been) to get people to stop drinking. Rather, I see my purpose in a more positive light. I want people to seek life's purpose, to confront questions of ultimate meaning, to recognize their innate nobility, and find their Beloved – sobriety is a side effect of this path. However, if asked why I choose abstinence, I'm happy to respond. I'm sure I do inadvertently upset people. Not because I'm rude, obstinate or accusatory, but because I question a socially entrenched addiction, one that usually requires no defence or consideration.

This work is an elongated version, therefore, of simpler points made in the moment, the real and deeper thoughts behind a brief dialogue.

'Don't knock it till you try it' vs. 'Look before you leap'

Often, my Bahá'í (and Christian and Muslim) friends say they feel handicapped by their lack of experience with drugs and alcohol. These friends never drank or used other drugs, nor directly grew up around alcohol or drug culture. So, people accuse them of judging without first-hand knowledge.

Their views are dismissed because they've never partaken. This is the cliché, 'Don't knock it till you try it.' Yet it contradicts another maxim: 'Look before you leap.' The first proverb says *Don't judge before experience*; the other *Don't jump in until you're informed*. Both proverbs apply at times in life. However, people can opt for 'Don't knock it till you try it' as a dismissal. Regardless, it is a bad argument.

We all readily understand the error being made. Consider: must we try heroin to deem it destructive? No. Should we take cocaine before deciding it's detrimental? Of course not. What of peyote, LSD, PCP, or crystal meth? This principle applies to endless possible experiences, many more ludicrous than those suggested so far. Surely, we don't have to kick dogs or kill dolphins before we argue against the practice, or experience street fighting or prostitution prior to deciding they're toxic. No great philosophical inquiry is required here – only honesty.

We don't need to run this grotesque experiential gauntlet to gauge an action's value. We can be more discerning. We can use reason – the same tool used to build skyscrapers, construct particle accelerators, and explore distant galaxies. We can, as well, employ our emotional and moral intelligence – the same organ we use to connect with others, build ethical philosophies, and establish universal human rights. This approach appears superior to demanding we sample every act prior to appraisal.

Sadly, in my earlier days, I made this argument all the time. I employed 'Don't knock it till you try it' and fully believed it made sense. I suppose I may have merely wanted it to.

Why down the drink?

We come to a key question: Why do people use alcohol or drugs? What makes them as seductive as a Siren's song? The answer is vital, and it is certainly important here for me to be fair. In dialogue, and in my own experience, the reasons are straightforward. People normally say:

* To have fun.
  * 'I like to have a good time, a laugh with the boys/girls. So, we're going out for a night on the town.'

* To ease stress.
  * 'I need to take a load off. I'm stressed. Let's split a case of beer.'

- To deal with hurt or depression.
  - ❖ 'I'm going through a rough patch right now. I need to get my mind off things. Do you want to grab a bottle of wine?'

- To ease social situations – the social lubricant.
  - ❖ 'It helps me lighten up. Let's have a couple of drinks before we go to the party. I could use a little *liquid courage*.'

The list isn't comprehensive. Yet it represents common reasons people drink. We drink to have fun or release pressure that built up throughout a tough week – or a tough day for some. Often, our inhibitions relax and we socialize easier with a touch of *liquid courage*, a dab of *social lubricant*.

Freedom – the fork in the road

If these be our reasons, a pivotal question for me arises: 'Do I *need* alcohol to achieve them?' A great deal hangs on the response. Suppose my answer is:

'Yes, I need alcohol to have fun, release stress, deal with pain in my life, and interact comfortably with others.'

What does this mean? If I *need* chemicals to achieve these goals, a close friend should have a sober conversation with me – pun intended. Essentially, if I say I *need* alcohol to relax, to have fun, to work my way through emotional times, I have lost my freedom in some real and important sense. It means I am dependent on a chemical, incapable of interacting naturally with the world.

I actually believe this state of affairs is quite common, more common than the number of those who would admit it. If so, I hope we take the inability to relate to the world without chemical crutches seriously. If someone is unable to navigate the world sober, they need strategies to become less reliant on the liquid crutch. Basically, they should see a drug and alcohol counsellor.

Conversely, if I don't *need* a chemical crutch, as many won't, there is genuine reason to rejoice. I do mean this sincerely. If I don't need external substances to have fun, deal with stress, cope with life's pain, or interact comfortably with others, I should congratulate myself or any other who could say the same. I am independent of the need for chemical props. I have taken off the cast, let the crutches fall and now walk freely.

I remember so many Friday nights *preparing* for the bar with an *adequate dose* of alcohol. I wanted to feel I was *on my game* and with the requisite *social lubricant*, the night flowed better. Preemptive liquor to alleviate social tension – to take the edge off, I'd say – always preceded any significant social setting. Otherwise, upon arriving – to lighten my mood – I'd quickly down *liquid courage*. I was more amusing and comical when I had a little *buzz.* Furthermore, I would *never* consider camping without a couple cases of beer or a few bottles of whisky. A long hike with friends was nonsense without at least a small bag of marijuana. But why? Why didn't I question this, for years?

We must confront this question of need. If you *need* chemicals to comfortably interact with people, to ease stress, to have fun, to deal with emotional, psychological, or physical pain, you *need* help. Don't passively accept this state of being. Conversely, if you are unfettered by the need for artificial supports – booze or drugs – I offer reasons for choosing full abstinence.

I argue why booze and drugs should be banished from our desires. Please note, I said our *desires*. Forget expelling it from society, homes, streets, or schools. These will result from the abolition of the need for chemical crutches. I wrote this book for human hearts, not legal institutions.

At this moment, I must stress one point: if you're addicted to alcohol or in the grip of other chemicals, this book may honestly not be for you. The arguments I pose can, at times, sound intense. I hope to raise our consciousness surrounding drug use, not offend any heart.

Love and hate

An important note: if you do use these substances, mind your thoughts and keep an eye on your emotions; your chemical dependence wants to maintain its existence.

In similar manner, abstainers may yearn to hear their view vindicated and make a conceptual error because of it. Bahá'u'lláh enjoins 'the independent investigation of truth'. This command is not confined to non-Bahá'ís. It's for all humanity, at all times. We must work long and hard to cultivate this principle. Be wary of accepting arguments because you like the conclusion.

Speaking of the true seeker, Bahá'u'lláh says:

> He must so cleanse his heart that no remnant of either love or hate may linger therein, lest that love blindly incline him to error, or that hate repel him away from the truth.[2]

A litmus test for freedom

If I don't *need* alcohol or drugs, this should mean I could easily forgo them. If offered a good reason, I'd drop them. I might like avocados, but not need them. If I learned, however, that avocados damage society and weaken me intellectually and spiritually, I could stop eating them immediately. I might enjoy snorkelling, but if I learned snorkels and flippers poisoned the water, killing many marine animals, I'd stop using them. I might like these things, but I also like other things that don't harm myself and others. So, goodbye avocados, snorkels and flippers. This is the litmus test for both freedom and justice; a test we'll carry out on this journey.

A flock of rebel sheep

Many see religious people as sheep: unquestioning creatures, sadly obedient, incapable of or unwilling to think for themselves. Often people will brush off religious abstainers in this way. They claim that by *denying* themselves the *right* to drink, religious people blindly obey the dictates of their Faith – an ironic accusation to me.

Surrounded by a drinking majority, being called a conformist is ironic. In the West, sobriety is an idiosyncrasy, a badge of oddity in most settings. Since my own choice to forgo alcohol, I represent a minority at most gatherings – usually a minority of one. Far from following the crowd, I walk in the opposite direction. Right or wrong, religiously motivated or not, which way *would* a conformist lean in our current culture? I suggest it is not towards abstinence. So, if a sheep, I'm a rebellious one indeed.

Modern blasphemies and the new taboos: The pendulum swing

Western culture represents itself as brash, brave and willing to broach any topic. It considers itself bold and unfettered by former taboos. No doubt, we have let go certain past taboos and prejudices. Yet we adopted new ones in their stead.

Though it is difficult to discern, we are not as open as we think. It seems, rather, we direct attention away from *our* taboos, like a body builder flexing his biceps to draw the gaze from spindly legs.

Yes, western culture discusses previously offensive topics. Yet naturally, in doing so, it often exalts character traits once thought ignoble. The Universal House of Justice calls attention to this tendency:

Various philosophies and theories have eroded precepts of right and wrong that govern personal behaviour. For some, relativism reigns and individuals are to determine their own moral preferences; others dismiss the very conception of personal morality, maintaining that any standard that restrains what is considered a natural impulse is harmful to the individual and ultimately to society. Self-indulgence, in the guise of expressing one's true nature, becomes the norm, even the touchstone of healthy living.[3]

Trying to avoid one extreme, we often fall, unaware, into the same trap. When we exalt self-indulgence, restraint will seem lowly, even unnatural. Elevate aggression or indifference, and peacefulness and passion plummet. Sex ascends, chastity falls; party-culture jumps, sobriety spirals; shallow entertainment flows and the joys of youth become paramount, long-term goals and the love of education ebb.

What results from this pendulum swing, this inversion of goals and aspirations? If pop music eulogizes female body parts, glorifies money, makes explicit sexual references, and nearly deifies club culture, what becomes taboo? I suggest the veneration of women, fidelity, the value of frugality and matters of import will then cause discomfort. We lie in the grip of 'modern blasphemies and new taboos', but a veneer of audacity hides them. The body builder flexes his biceps, and all I see are his spaghetti legs.

How to clear a room – the good, the true, the just, the beautiful

If my perspective seems extreme, and I understand it might, I propose a difficult experiment. The challenge is not methodological, but psychological. Logistically, it's a breeze. Socially however, you may find it far more difficult. But that is my point. Here it is.

To rapidly clear a room, scream, 'Fire!' Another technique exists, but the evacuation happens more slowly. Instead of panicked running, people suddenly go to the bathroom, recall an urgent task, or a phone call they forgot to make. If not evacuation, you may experience abrupt and awkward topic changes. The method? Speak passionately of the good, the true, the just, and the beautiful. I realize I may sound cynical here, but don't brush this aside just yet.

To carry out the experiment, randomly select 30 days on your calendar. Divide them into equal parts of 15. Then, choose various social settings: the lunchroom at work, coffee with a friend, dinner with family, a chat with your boss, socializing with friends, a dinner party – any and all of them.

On 15 days, choose a cynical stance, complain, express lower aims, or speak negatively. For example, if male, grumble about women; if female, complain about men. Criticize your wife or husband. Talk about your sexual attraction to people other than your spouse. Bash some politicians. Slam an ethnicity or two (but remember to begin with, 'I'm not racist but . . .'). State that an entire religious group is dangerous, or all religions generally. Call the UN goals 'utopian', reject any responsibility to help the less fortunate. Proclaim you don't have money to help; then, shortly after, talk about wanting to buy something frivolous. Talk about how you deserve a new car, TV, cellphone, truck, computer, new clothes, a bigger house, etc. Assert you don't have time to help others, or investigate deep questions. Then, (again shortly after) talk about watching television, playing video games, or scanning social media. Talk about liquors you like, be it wine, beer, or rum. And wait for disagreement, discomfort, or open opposition. Also, log how often people propose counter-examples, exceptions to the rule.

On the other 15 days, choose optimism, praise people, extol noble goals, pay tribute to discipline and loyalty, to the good, the true, the just and the beautiful. If male, praise women's nobility, and recall their unsung contribution to history. If female, honour good men, those who fight for justice and righteousness. Speak – at length – of your wife or husband's noble qualities, of how you won the lottery by marrying them. Praise fidelity, expressing your undying devotion to your spouse; acknowledge your lower desires, but also your fight against disloyal sexual thoughts. Praise politicians who seek to aid humankind, the good intentions of those with whom you nonetheless disagree, who sacrifice their time to better civilization. Speak on how our global system sets certain ethnic groups up to fail but how all of us are a global family. Proclaim racial differences an illusion, stating we are the waves of one sea, rays of one light, flowers of one garden. Speak for the vast majority of Muslims, how their Faith is beautiful and misunderstood, their aims peaceful, their contribution to global history immense. Declare that we could – if we wanted – achieve the UN goals. Affirm our duty to help starving people in other countries; speak of your frustrations with poverty, war, child soldiery, and the sexual exploitation of women; state that *we all have* enough time and money to spare. Praise detachment from worldly things, and how we can sacrifice our wants for the needs of others. Talk about sobriety and why it's a noble choice. And wait for discomfort, disagreement or open opposition. Note how often people propose counter-examples, exceptions to the rule. If nothing else, note your own sentiments and anxieties around introducing *these* topics as opposed to the cynical or mundane.

Perform this experiment, and you'll find many modern blasphemies and new taboos. Sadly, I assume that for many readers the experiment is unnecessary. They're aware which topics will elicit greater discomfort, disapproval or disagreement. For others,

I believe you'll find that bringing up truly elevated discussions proves challenging. Cynical, negative, rough or mundane topics often flow more easily in discourse. The good, the true, the just and the beautiful – these themes rock the emotional, psychological and spiritual boat too much.

But not all social groups are identical. Some settings prove more amenable to elevated discourse, some positively hostile. No doubt, when I worked in the social service field, nobler topics arose more easily. When I worked on shipping docks, in construction or in education – not so much. Yet, if you move in social circles that encourage (or even accept) nobler topics, I am delighted for you; be grateful.

If I sound *cynical, negative* or *gruff*, please perform the experiment. I would happily be wrong on this point, and yes, I have tested this myself. Yet, pointing out these taboos – I am aware – implies a character flaw. It smells of superiority. I may have, therefore, committed a grave cultural sin: being judgemental.

Judging judgemental people

Of course, the Bahá'í Faith – as with all God's Messages – cautions against fault-finding:

> Each of us is responsible for one life only, and that is our own. Each of us is immeasurably far from being 'perfect as our heavenly Father is perfect' and the task of perfecting our own life and character is one that requires all our attention, our will-power and energy. If we allow our attention and energy to be taken up in efforts to keep others right and remedy their faults, we are wasting precious time. We are like ploughmen, each of whom has his team to manage and his plough to direct, and in order to keep his furrow straight he must keep his eye on his goal and concentrate on his own task. If he

looks to this side and that to see how Tom and Harry are getting on and to criticize their ploughing, then his own furrow will assuredly become crooked.[4]

We cannot cultivate our character while preoccupied with others' errors. Our goal should be to rectify our own conduct. If we focus on others, we stray off course.

At the same time, we speak for love and justice, global education and global unity, the eradication of prejudice and the building of communities. Consequently, their antitheses – injustice, ignorance, disunity, bias and civil decline – express shadows of our true reality. Hence, when our goals are up, we necessarily see what is down: understand darkness, and you know light, to perceive one is to know the other. If something is worthy of praise its opposite cannot be.

To navigate this landscape, we must discern between being judgemental and being discerning, between proclaiming someone degraded, worthless or evil and judging an action or viewpoint wrong. These are not identical. 'Abdu'l-Bahá states:

> We must love all with love of the heart. Some are ignorant; they must be trained and educated. One is sick; he must be healed. Another is as a child; we must assist him to attain maturity. We must not detest him who is ailing, neither shun him, scorn nor curse him, but care for him with the utmost kindness and tenderness. An infant must not be treated with disdain simply because it is an infant. Our responsibility is to train, educate and develop it in order that it may advance toward maturity.[5]

We must love the ignorant, the sick, the immature. How else could we choose to sacrifice our time to educate, heal and nurture them? Yet, this does not mean we proclaim the ignorant to be wise; the sick, healthy; the juvenile, mature. To do so would be untruthful. Even more, we must diagnose a person as sick, recognize they could be healthier, if we are ever to offer a remedy.

At present, our culture perceives '*being judgemental*' as a horrid moral failing. If you disapprove of certain actions, many people get upset. We will quickly judge the judgemental. The error flows from a beautiful desire to defend others, but also from a flawed belief: that to recognize darkness, we must proclaim someone worthless or evil. I would suggest medicine to a sick person for the same reasons I challenge a racist's belief.

As a father of two, I don't consider my children worthless or evil because their actions are improper or harmful at times. They need to be taught life's higher paths, to be guided to greater goals. To do so, I must teach them to be discerning. I *want* them to deem musical proficiency more important than television.

We *must* judge people's actions. When I teach my children to greet people with warmth and courtesy, they learn that doing so in a cold, rude manner is wrong. When I tell them to be educated, ignorance takes the lower rung on the value hierarchy. I proclaim compassion a noble trait; they view indifference as blameworthy. When teaching them to respect the biosphere, I degrade environmentally toxic behaviours. Raising virtuous and progressive children logically entails this process. Naturally, if I nurture them into noble beings, they'll disapprove of rude, violent, harmful or hateful behaviours – I sure hope they will.

Consider honestly: how *could* I stop my children from judging others' actions and beliefs? I suggest the answer is quite simple; I could lower their opinion of humanity. If I reduce their expectations of self and others, they could approve no matter what someone did; they could see wholesomeness in any act. They could also, therefore, do anything and feel appropriate and decent. No judgement needed because everything is permissible.

But I neither can nor should do this. I want my children to believe they have great potential, to see humanity as intrinsically noble. I want them to inspire others, urging them to leave the valley of *what is*, for the peaks of *what could be*. I long for them to fix their eyes on their capacity, and climb.

I suggest we are culturally confused. We obscure the difference between *looking up* and *looking down*. Fixating on the latter hinders humanity; the path of human potential must look to the former. But our confusion infects discussions about conduct and nobility. Let me explain . . .

Once, after discussing alcohol, my friend said he'd feel uncomfortable drinking around me. I asked why. He replied, 'Because I know you'd look down on me.'

I replied, 'But why didn't you say, "because you have a high opinion of who I could be"? Why express it in terms of *looking down* on you, as opposed to *looking up* at your potential? Why not see me *believing in you* instead of *judging you*?' My reply startled him; his perception flipped.

I don't look down on people who use chemicals for fun; I believe we're powerful and capable. I admire the dignified creature waiting inside. Humanity's improper acts don't generate my sadness; rather, it is our caged inherent nobility that causes my grief. If I see a potentially beautiful artist doodling stickmen, I sigh. I'm not looking down and judging; I look up at potential, and hope, and pray.

As a 40-something adult, I discern between wholesome and unwholesome facets of my own character; I am ignorant, sick and immature in many ways. I do not, however, see myself as evil, vile or unworthy of compassion. I look at what I can become, and judge thereby my current state. This is how I progress, and how humanity always advances.

All religions summon us to spiritual distinction, to raise our standards above what is. 'Abdu'l-Bahá states:

I desire distinction for you. The Bahá'ís must be distinguished from others of humanity. But this distinction must not depend upon wealth – that they should become more affluent than other people. I do not desire for you financial distinction. It is not an ordinary distinction I desire: not scientific, commercial, industrial distinction. For you I desire spiritual distinction; that is, you must become eminent and distinguished in morals. In the love of God you must become distinguished from all else. You must become distinguished for loving humanity; for unity and accord; for love and justice. In brief, you must become distinguished in all the virtues of the human world – for faithfulness and sincerity, for justice and fidelity, for firmness and steadfastness; for philanthropic deeds and service to the human world; for love toward every human being, for unity and accord with all people, for removing prejudices and promoting international peace. Finally, you must become distinguished for heavenly illumination and acquiring the bestowals of God. I desire this distinction for you. This must be the point of distinction among you.[6]

How can we seek distinction, and hope to avoid noticing difference? It's impossible. We must, therefore, seek such distinction but maintain our love and respect for all humankind. To achieve this, we need to *heal* and *educate* our culture's values. We must help humanity see the difference between proposing nobler values, and proclaiming those who don't do them (or do them yet) as degraded.

Currently, we often find vulgar and insensitive people more acceptable than those who condemn vulgarity and insensitivity. People judge judgemental people – intensely so at times. Yet this flows from the confusion between seeing an act as wrong, and pronouncing a person innately depraved. This difference must, at least, be seen.

To clear this confusion, we can help people see that belief in our beauty makes us cheer for what we can be, makes us hope for a higher path, makes us say, 'We can do better.'

Now, we've packed our bags with perceptual provisions for the journey. We will 'look before we leap', because we *can*, without experience, judge an action's worth. We will watch for the veil of normalcy, lest familiarity disguise detriment. We'll be wary of *new taboos,* lest prior attachments or entrenched cultural norms cause shock when we question pervasive if not precious customs. We will remember that, if free from chemical dependence, a *good enough* reason should suffice, and this will be *the litmus test for justice and our own freedom.* As well, we seek peaks of potential and cannot, therefore, ignore the valleys below – though harsh judgement and condemnation we will avoid. I trust you will now better understand why, if we do not *need* these drugs, we should consider letting them go.

Now, let's begin our tour with the *Temple of the Body*.

2

The Temple of the Body

The Bahá'í Writings praise the grace and purity of the body; God summons us to honour the *Temple of the Body*:

> Bestow Thou in all things purity and cleanliness upon the people of Bahá. Grant that they be freed from all defilement, and released from all addictions. Save them from committing any repugnant act, unbind them from the chains of every evil habit, that they may live pure and free, wholesome and cleanly, worthy to serve at Thy Sacred Threshold and fit to be related to their Lord. Deliver them from intoxicating drinks and tobacco, save them, rescue them, from this opium that bringeth on madness, suffer them to enjoy the sweet savors of holiness, that they may drink deep of the mystic cup of heavenly love and know the rapture of being drawn ever closer unto the Realm of the All-Glorious. For it is even as Thou hast said: 'All that thou hast in thy cellar will not appease the thirst of my love – bring me, O cupbearer, of the wine of the spirit a cup as full as the sea!'[1]

Culturally, we admire health and strength. The Bahá'í Writings laud these characteristics as well. God asks that we maintain harmonious and pure physical temples. But what of alcohol?

. . . Isn't it healthy at times? People often cite alcohol's health benefits to justify drinking. I regularly encounter the argument. It generally appears, however, late in the dialogue.

Yet, if it's so common, why didn't I mention it before? I listed reasons people drink; why the omission? I omitted it for good reason: it isn't a genuine motivation. This may appear confusing: if I acknowledge that people offer the health rationale, why call it fake?

Have you ever heard the following statements?

- 'I'm going for a couple of beers with friends, because I'm concerned about my blood pressure.'

- 'It's Friday night, so I'm heading to the pub. I dedicate Friday nights to heart health.'

- 'A bottle of wine would go well with this dinner. I need to offset the fatty content of this steak and fries.'

If these statements sound silly (and they should), I assume the reason why is apparent. No one drinks *for* health reasons. Or rather, I've *never* met a person who does. People drink because they like drinking. Nevertheless, the health justification persists. Why? We seek to justify our habits. Of course, some may genuinely think it's true, even if it's more of a hope. But the health rationale is *always* an afterthought, *never* a primary reason. That's why I didn't list it earlier.

A simple concept

You drop by your friend Bob's house for lunch. He answers the door and invites you in. Immediately, you notice he's acting odd. He seems a little off-balance. His eyes are glassy. Brushing it off, you grab a seat and ask what he's been up to lately. He begins talking, his speech slightly slurred, his thoughts muddled; he's noticeably confused. He changes topics without warning and frequently repeats himself. You continue talking, unconcerned by his glazed eyes, stumbling tongue and gently bobbing head. Sure, it's a bit early in the day, but after all, this is Bob.

Suddenly, you feel dizzy and recognize your own thoughts seem jumbled. You decide to stand up, wobbling slightly as you do. Then, you notice a strange smell in the room. How did you miss it?

Instantly, you grab Bob's arm and pull him toward the door, ignoring his mumbled objections. You clumsily drag him outside, sit him down, and fumble with your phone to call an ambulance. In moments, Bob is unconscious on the lawn.

Minutes later, the ambulance pulls up. They put an oxygen mask on you and your friend, and while one paramedic takes his vitals, the other questions you. You describe what happened, and the paramedic asks why you didn't get him out faster. You shake your head in frustration, 'I thought he'd been drinking. I assumed he just started a little earlier than usual.'

The moral of the story: No one needs health studies to prove alcohol harms the body; all you need is Bob.

Observe anyone drink; this suffices. They lose their coordination. It impairs their memory. They repeat themselves, slur their speech, display peculiar emotional responses, and act in ways they never would sober.

Their ability to function – physically, mentally and emotionally – deteriorates with each drink. Do we need additional evidence that alcohol damages the Temple of the Body? Look what it does to it.

Bob's story is far from fanciful. First aid responders must recognize alcohol's effect on the brain. I am a first aid attendant. And when surveying patients, I must assess their level of consciousness. In the standard *Occupational First Aid: A Reference and Training Manual* written by WorkSafeBC in Canada, we are told:

> Any patient under the influence of drugs or alcohol who has sustained any trauma to the head or face and has an altered level of consciousness must be assumed to have sustained a brain injury until proven otherwise.[2]

> A patient intoxicated with alcohol may also have a serious head injury. The Attendant must never attribute a patient's level of consciousness to alcohol or drugs when there is evidence of head injury or other medical conditions (e.g. diabetes).[3]

Why can't a first aid attendant assume alcohol or drugs caused a diminished level of consciousness? . . . Because intoxication mimics a brain injury. So, you can mistake a drunk person for someone who's had a serious head injury – or vice versa. Please pause to consider why this is.

In addition, WorkSafeBC references carbon monoxide poisoning. A person 'may appear drunk', but is a victim of 'poisoning by inhalation'.[4] That is why you thought Bob was drunk – he'd been poisoned by toxic fumes. So, if on Friday night, you see a friend acting 'drunk', he might not be intoxicated. Possibly, someone bashed him in the head, and he has brain trauma. Or, maybe he's poisoned – exposed to a toxic chemical.

Rather than prolong the analogy, I'll be frank. Your friend has both medical issues. He has sustained *brain injury* from a *toxic chemical:* alcohol.

If this was another substance – and it *wasn't* a celebrated pastime – everyone would think booze was a toxic chemical. Someone not veiled by normalcy, unhindered by the desire to drink, would never deny booze damages the body.

Before reading on, consider: if alcohol were discovered today, would anyone think it safe? Would anyone hope we adopt it as commonplace in numerous social gatherings?

Pointless not poignant statistics

Research on alcohol's health effects won't please its admirers. Nevertheless, it won't aid my argument either, because I don't think anyone drinks for health. Thus, if I remove evidence the jury didn't care about, it won't sway the verdict. Yet, for those who do wonder, we'll take a look. Before doing so, many people – at this and subsequent points along our journey – will think, 'But I don't drink that much' or 'But I don't get drunk, rowdy or aggressive'. The issue of being a 'responsible drinker' will be dealt with later. For now, let's simply examine research on alcohol and health.

A quick query

In my exploration, I purposely didn't even *attempt* to be academic. Rather, I want to show what anyone with a computer – should they wish to know – would find with a brief survey. In short, I *Googled* it.

The sources I use below are:

+ Harvard School of Public Health, Harvard University
+ Mayo Clinic, a major nonprofit health research organization
+ The World Health Organization (WHO)
+ The American Heart Association (AHA)
+ *Berkeley Wellness*, a website of the School of Public Health at University of California, Berkeley
+ The United States National Institute on Alcohol Abuse and Alcoholism
+ The Canadian Centre for Substance Abuse (CCSA)

- The Canadian Centre for Addiction and Mental Health (CAMH)
- The United Kingdom Stroke Association
- UK Government official website
- Institute for Alcohol Studies (IAS), United Kingdom

The elephant and the mouse

A disclaimer: I don't stand 100% behind the data presented; I acknowledge that vested interests could manipulate the data. These agencies may skew statistics or falsify information to create a caricature of alcohol. They might want to discredit the benefits of booze. Correspondingly, the alcohol industry generates unimaginable wealth, so it seeks to promote our culture's preferred chemical pastime. It's their business.

I suggest that if data manipulation occurs, therefore, it is probably in alcohol's favour. The alcohol industry is a multi-billion-dollar elephant; the abstinence lobby, an emaciated mouse. Either way, let us see what the numbers are . . .

The benefits of booze

Do any studies find health benefits from alcohol? Yes. The Harvard School of Public Health, on their site *The Nutrition Source*, states:

> More than 100 prospective studies show an inverse association between moderate drinking and risk of heart attack, ischemic (clot-caused) stroke, peripheral vascular disease, sudden cardiac death, and death from all cardiovascular causes. The effect is fairly consistent, corresponding to a 25 percent to 40 percent reduction in risk.
>
> The benefits of moderate drinking aren't limited to the

heart. In the Nurses' Health Study, the Health Professionals Follow-up Study, and other studies, gallstones and type 2 diabetes were less likely to occur in moderate drinkers than in non-drinkers.[5]

The Mayo Clinic reports that

Moderate alcohol consumption may provide some health benefits. It may:
- Reduce your risk of developing heart disease
- Reduce your risk of dying of a heart attack
- Possibly reduce your risk of strokes, particularly ischemic strokes
- Lower your risk of gallstones
- Possibly reduce your risk of diabetes[6]

Yet in the same article, it cautions:

Even so, the evidence about the possible health benefits of alcohol isn't certain, and alcohol may not benefit everyone who drinks.[7]

The 2011 *Global Status Report on Alcohol and Health* by the World Health organization (WHO), a United Nations agency, also speaks of possible benefits:

Light to moderate drinking can have a beneficial impact on morbidity and mortality for ischaemic heart disease and ischaemic stroke. However, the beneficial cardioprotective effect of drinking disappears with heavy drinking occasions . . . light to moderate drinkers experienced no protective effect if they reported at least one heavy drinking occasion per month. Moreover, alcohol consumption has detrimental

effects on hypertension, cardiac dysrhythmias and haemor-
rhagic stroke, regardless of the drinking pattern.[8]

While admitting potential benefits, the WHO says they disappear with 'one heavy drinking occasion per month'. With *one*
episode, you will experience 'no protective effect'. Further, the
paragraph lists dangers – hypertension, cardiac dysrhythmias and
stroke – saying these occur 'regardless of the drinking pattern'.

The Berkeley Wellness Centre, at University of California,
Berkeley's School of Public Health, offers the following:

> Some research suggests that daily (or almost daily) drinking
> is best for the heart, others that drinking every other day is
> enough to get the benefits. Some studies have found that all
> it takes is half a standard drink a day.[9]

> In the U.S. a 'drink' is 5 ounces of wine, 12 ounces of beer
> or 1.5 ounces of 80-proof liquor, which all contain about 14
> grams of pure alcohol (ethanol).[10]

So you can achieve the *possible* benefits with 2.5 ounces of wine,
6 ounces of beer, or 0.75 ounces of hard liquor, or in layman
terms:

- ½ a can of beer
- ¼ an average glass of wine
- ½ of a small mixed drink

Can you collect your daily wine, wait until the weekend, and
drop the whole dose? No, you can't. Can you save up your ½
cans of beer until the weekend, and get a buzz while you get
healthy? No.

It is not okay to abstain during the week and then consume your whole weekly 'quota' on the weekend. This is known as episodic heavy drinking, a term that has replaced 'binge drinking'. Heavy drinking, even confined to special occasions, is dangerous.[11]

This rules out Western drinking patterns. No one can justify 'a night out' by citing alcohol's health benefits. You can't get drunk – or even *tipsy* – following this guidance. In fact, if you're buzzed or tipsy, you're harming yourself.

Since we're discussing heart health, let's turn to the American Heart Association (AHA):

Some researchers have suggested that the benefit may be due to wine, especially red wine.[12]

For wine drinkers, you must, however, read on:

Some of these components may be found in other foods such as grapes or red grape juice.[13]

. . . even if they were protective, antioxidants can be obtained from many fruits and vegetables, including red grape juice.[14]

The AHA says you can gain the health benefits from grapes or grape juice. Even more, they say:

The linkage reported in many of these studies may be due to other lifestyle factors rather than alcohol. Such factors may include increased physical activity, and a diet high in fruits and vegetables and lower in saturated fats. No direct comparison trials have been done to determine the specific effect of wine or other alcohol on the risk of developing heart disease or stroke.[15]

The benefits come from 'other lifestyle factors rather than alcohol' such as exercise and diet. Also, the AHA claims they've seen no trials comparing these other factors to the effect of alcohol alone.

Regardless, they finish with the following recommendation:

> . . . the American Heart Association does not recommend drinking wine or any other form of alcohol to gain these potential benefits. The AHA does recommend that to reduce your risk you should talk to your doctor about lowering your cholesterol and lowering high blood pressure, controlling your weight, getting enough physical activity and following a healthy diet. There is no scientific proof that drinking wine or any other alcoholic beverage can replace these conventional measures.[16]

In summary, alcohol *may* benefit you, but this can't justify getting buzzed or tipsy – let alone drunk; if you feel alcohol's effect, you've had too much. Drink over the amounts prescribed, you'll damage your body. Even if you strictly limit your intake, a single night of heavy drinking negates any possible benefits. And since you can achieve the health benefits through exercise, eating well, and controlling your weight, don't drink for health reasons. Consequently, the health justification fails. It doesn't get better, as we shall see below.

Don't drink for health

Should you start drinking for health? What does the Mayo Clinic say?

> Certainly, you don't have to drink any alcohol, and if you currently don't drink, don't start drinking for the possible health

benefits. In some cases, it's safest to avoid alcohol entirely – the possible benefits don't outweigh the risks.[17]

What about the American Heart Association?

Drinking more alcohol increases such dangers as alcoholism, high blood pressure, obesity, stroke, breast cancer, suicide and accidents . . . Given these and other risks, the American Heart Association cautions people NOT to start drinking . . . if they do not already drink alcohol.[18]

How about the Canadian Centre for Addiction and Mental Health?

Although drinking small amounts of alcohol a day has been found to offer some protection against heart attack and stroke, there are still more effective ways to protect your health. These include eating a healthy diet, staying active, getting enough sleep, and having regular health checks as recommended by your doctor.[19]

Basically, avoid alcohol for health reasons. Don't begin drinking, the dangers outweigh the benefits. But even if potential benefits exist, people fail to mention *whom* it's supposed to benefit.

Missing the mark: Menopause and middle age

Who is alcohol supposed to be good for? The University of California, Berkeley says:

Keep in mind, too, that there's little or no cardiovascular benefit for premenopausal women or for men under 40, since they are at much lower risk.[20]

The Canadian Centre for Addiction and Mental Health realizes most people are misinformed about who benefits from alcohol:

These health benefits apply mainly to people over 45. In most cases, one drink of alcohol every other day is enough to obtain these benefits.[21]

And the Harvard School of Public Health says:

The benefits and risks of moderate drinking change over a lifetime. In general, risks exceed benefits until middle age, when cardiovascular disease begins to account for an increasingly large share of the burden of disease and death.

- For a 30-year-old man, the increased risk of alcohol-related accidents outweighs the possible heart-related benefits of moderate alcohol consumption.
- For a 60-year-old man, a drink a day may offer protection against heart disease that is likely to outweigh potential harm (assuming he isn't prone to alcoholism).
- For a 60-year-old woman, the benefit/risk calculations are trickier. Ten times more women die each year from heart disease (460,000) than from breast cancer (41,000). However, studies show that women are far more afraid of developing breast cancer than heart disease, something that must be factored into the equation.[22]

So, if you're under 60 years old: don't drink. If you're over 60 and male, have a ½ drink a day. It *may* help you. If you're female, your risk of breast cancer increases; factor this into your decision. Best option in both cases: eat healthy and exercise.

In my experience, those who offer the 'health rationale' don't fit this description: over 60 or past menopause. They all miss the mark. I'm sure as I get older that will change; I'll know more post-menopausal women and men over 60. At that time, if they drink, I'll ask if they recently began having a ½ glass of wine a day. If not, the rationale still fails.

Negating the benefits – the dangers of the drink

I'm sure this has become tedious, and likely unsurprising for the most part. Nevertheless, let's examine the data and become earnestly aware of alcohol's negative effects, starting with the Harvard School of Public Health:

> Heavy drinking is a major cause of preventable death in most countries. In the U.S., alcohol is implicated in about half of fatal traffic accidents. Heavy drinking can damage the liver and heart, harm an unborn child, increase the chances of developing breast and some other cancers, contribute to depression and violence, and interfere with relationships.[23]

In the section titled 'Folate and alcohol', they state:

> Alcohol blocks the absorption of folate and inactivates folate in the blood and tissues. It's possible that this interaction may be how alcohol consumption increases the risk of breast, colon, and other cancers.[24]

Of course, they continue, 'Alcohol abuse costs more than $185 billion dollars a year', but we'll consider that social impact in the next chapter. Alcohol's role in breast cancer, however, sounds chilling:

> There is convincing evidence that alcohol consumption increases the risk of breast cancer. In a combined analysis of

six large prospective studies involving more than 320,000 women, researchers found that having two or more drinks a day increased the chances of developing breast cancer as much as 41 percent.[25]

According to Harvard, alcohol costs taxpayers a scandalous amount of money. But a 41% greater chance of breast cancer is a terrifying price for a couple glasses of wine. And many women I know drink 'two or more' glasses of wine with dinner.

In February 2011, the World Health Organization (WHO) posed, and then answered, the following question:

Q: Is harmful use of alcohol a public health problem?
A: Yes, the harmful use of alcohol is an important public health problem. It impacts people and societies in many ways.

It is well known that there is a causal relationship between alcohol consumption and a range of mental and behavioural disorders, including alcohol dependence, other non-communicable conditions such as liver diseases, some cancers, cardiovascular diseases, as well as injuries resulting from violence and road accidents . . . More than this, harmful use of alcohol creates considerable negative health and social consequences for people other than the drinker . . .

Harmful use of alcohol is a causal factor in more than 200 diseases and injuries. In 2012, 5.1% of the global disease burden was due to the harmful use of alcohol, and an estimated 3.3 million people died from alcohol related conditions that year.[26]

The WHO lists numerous public health problems associated with alcohol. If it is a 'causal factor in more than 200 diseases and injuries' the WHO naturally views this as 'an important public health problem' worldwide. But it's difficult to imagine 3.3 million deaths in a single year.

I live in Vancouver, Canada. Metro Vancouver houses over two million people. Pause to truly contemplate this please. I imagine waking up to the sound of wind blowing, birds chirping, bees buzzing – and nothing else. No cars rushing, no radios, no stereos, no sirens in the distance – no people talking, nothing. Why? Alcohol's global burden wiped out my city. *Actually, two-thirds of my province.* If this were an earthquake or plague, the entire globe would mourn. Yet we don't, because this is how we have fun – a *recreational* drug.

The University of California, Berkeley's Wellness Centre continues the tragic tale:

A new study published in the *American Journal of Public Health* estimates that alcohol causes 3 to 4 percent of all cancer deaths in the U.S. (about 19,500 deaths each year). Most of the cancer-related deaths in women are from breast cancer, while most in men are from oral and esophageal cancer. The researchers estimate that at least half of the deaths occur in people consuming three or more drinks a day; about 30 percent in those averaging fewer than 1.5 drinks a day. On average, alcohol-related cancer deaths shorten lives by about 18 years.[27]

The WHO's *Global Status Report on Alcohol and Health* of 2011 revealed:

Alcohol consumption is the world's third largest risk factor for disease and disability; in middle-income countries, it is the greatest risk. Alcohol is a causal factor in 60 types of diseases and injuries and a component cause in 200 others. Almost 4% of all deaths worldwide are attributed to alcohol, greater than deaths caused by HIV/AIDS, violence or tuberculosis. Alcohol is also associated with many serious social issues, including violence, child neglect and abuse, and absenteeism in the workplace.

Yet, despite all these problems, the harmful use of alcohol remains a low priority in public policy, including in health policy. Many lesser health risks have higher priority.[28]

So, the WHO ranks alcohol a greater threat than AIDS, tuberculosis – or violence! It then points out that we give lesser risks a 'higher priority'. Why? The answer, I trust, is now obvious. Alcohol is entrenched in culture; we relish our spirits, lagers and wines. We have no personal stake or attachment to TB, but we certainly do to beer and wine.

The WHO Report continues:

The harmful use of alcohol is a particularly grave threat to men. It is the leading risk factor for death in males ages 15–59, mainly due to injuries, violence and cardiovascular diseases.[29]

Cancer: alcohol consumption has been identified as carcinogenic for the following cancer categories: cancers of the colorectum, female breast, larynx, liver, esophagus, oral cavity and pharynx. The higher the consumption of alcohol, the greater the risk for these cancers: even the consumption of two drinks per day causes an increased risk for some cancers, such as breast cancer.[30]

In 2006, over a decade ago, the Institute for Alcohol Studies in the United Kingdom reported to the European Commission:

This health impact is seen across a wide range of conditions, including 17,000 deaths per year due to road traffic accidents (1 in 3 of all road traffic fatalities), 27,000 accidental deaths, 2,000 homicides (4 in 10 of all murders and manslaughters),

10,000 suicides (1 in 6 of all suicides), 45,000 deaths from liver cirrhosis, 50,000 cancer deaths, of which 11,000 are female breast cancer deaths, and 17,000 deaths due to neuropsychiatric conditions as well as 200,000 episodes of depression . . .[31]

With this in mind, we can understand why the WHO Report speaks on the significance of abstinence:

> Abstention from alcohol is very important in the global picture on alcohol consumption; it is one of the strongest predictors of the magnitude of alcohol-attributable burden of disease and injuries in populations. Obviously, lifetime abstention from alcohol means exemption from personal alcohol-attributable disease, injury and death. Because abstention is so prevalent in the world, any diminution in abstention trends could have a big impact on the global burden of disease caused by the harmful use of alcohol.[32]

At this point, I remind you that I don't stand by all the research. Rather, I offer information anyone could discover, and at least consider. I wanted to examine the 'health justification' for alcohol, to see if the average person would find data that calls it into question. I chose medical and educational organizations. In them, we read that alcohol is dangerous, unhealthy, and as we shall see later (though less often discussed), economically devastating.

But I don't think people drink for health reasons. We drink because we like to let go, have fun, take a load off or navigate social situations bolstered by liquid courage. Booze appears to help us do that. We drink as well, in some cases, because recreational drug use is the norm.

Even if true

Remember, even if we find a legitimate medical use for alcohol, a doctor should prescribe it, and a pharmacist administer it. Given the destructive global impact, it should be controlled by health professionals. Treat it as a medicine, not a pastime. Morphine is useful in health-related situations, but we don't sell it at corner stores. We should keep any drug responsible for a worldwide pandemic behind counters, not stocked in fridges.

Let us please drop the health rationale. If anyone offers health as a justification for alcohol, ask this question: 'If you drink for health, would you opt for a pill rather than the pub?'

If honest, people would answer 'No'. And this response tracks actual drinking patterns. Normal drinking patterns far exceed guidelines alleging alcohol's benefits. Half a beer on Monday may be beneficial; a dozen on Friday, detrimental. Half a glass of wine may help on the road to health; a bottle is a barricade.

As a parting quotation, I give you the Government of the United Kingdom:

We know that:

- 83% of those who regularly drink above the guidelines do not think their drinking is putting their long-term health at risk.
- Whereas most smokers wish to quit, only 18% of people who drink above the lower-risk guidelines say they actually wish to change their behaviour.[33]

You will not find our drive to drink in the data; our culture drinks *in spite* of the data – and common sense. But I think we all knew that, deep down, before reading this section.

'The point' and 'the bottom bar'

'The point' is a brief chapter summary and the essential argument. 'The bottom bar' is what abstinence's challengers should concede at this point. In short, the bottom bar is a genuine response to the point.

The point. People don't drink alcohol for their health. Health is an afterthought, a justification, not a genuine motivation. Alcohol harms your health. Nearly everyone (to some degree) already knows this, even if unaware of the severity. Yet, if possible benefits exist, they can't justify our culture's drinking practices. You can't get 'a buzz' or feel 'tipsy' (let alone drunk) and be on the road to health. Alcohol defaces the Temple of the Body. We should, therefore, cast it aside as an impediment to optimum health.

The bottom bar. If you still drink alcohol, congratulate abstainers; it's a path of physical harmony, and they try to honour the Temple of the Body. As Bahá'u'lláh revealed:

> Beware of using any substance that induceth sluggishness and torpor in the human temple and inflicteth harm upon the body. We, verily, desire for you naught save what shall profit you, and to this bear witness all created things, had ye but ears to hear.[34]

3

The Temple of the Heart

Simple questions

Our species can manifest profound altruism, awaken deep compassion, and summon the will to sacrifice. In our noble moments, we unite to alleviate suffering, undertake heroic social projects, and cast off cultural conventions that impede our collective evolution. Bahá'u'lláh proclaims this the purpose of existence:

> All men have been created to carry forward an ever-advancing civilization. The Almighty beareth Me witness: To act like the beasts of the field is unworthy of man. Those virtues that befit his dignity are forbearance, mercy, compassion and loving-kindness towards all the peoples and kindreds of the earth.[1]

Belief in humanity's inherent dignity drives social evolution and offers the simplest argument for sobriety. Ask yourself this question: Would an ever-advancing civilization – guided by forbearance, mercy and compassion, dedicated to progress and noble pursuits – cling to alcohol and drug use?

Considered with open hearts and minds, I think we must answer, 'No.'

If we hesitate here, I suggest it is emotional attachment, not critical thought, that restrains the tongue. Consider the inverse question: Would a utopian society, after discovering alcohol and learning of its effects, choose it? I can't imagine a reason why.

I believe, as with health, the issue is far from complex. Imagine: You ask the local fire department, women's shelters, police force, rehabilitation centres, judicial system, counselling and emergency room personnel this question:

'Would you have less work if alcohol and drugs vanished from society?'

How do you think they would respond? Would the police officer say, 'We'd see no reduction in assaults, vandalism or thefts'? Would the women's shelter staff state, 'Abuse would not dwindle, and families would be no better off'? Would nurses and emergency personnel proclaim, 'Our days would see no change'? Or do you think they might expect lay-offs?

Do you believe any would answer, 'No. Levels of violence, property damage, physical and emotional suffering of individual and families would not change if drugs and alcohol disappeared'?

I don't think anyone believes this. No one thinks these professionals would be *less busy* in any major (or minor) city. I believe the issue is clear. We will, however, undertake an exploration of the social impact of recreational chemicals.

A brief inquiry

I speak mostly on alcohol – as opposed to other drugs – because our culture ignores (or remains unaware of) the damage it inflicts. As I've said, I believe we all know – to some degree – that alcohol harms humanity. As well, think, if eating plums injured our planet to the same degree, they would be a thing of the past. Some people, however, do not know alcohol's social costs: social, financial, physical, emotional and psychological.

Out of obligation (or convention), we'll survey liquor's social consequences. Once again, as with the health statistics, I don't claim the data is impeccable. My sole point is this: we find evidence readily available that alcohol leaves considerable destruction in its wake.

As with the Temple of the Body, I performed a simple Internet search. Once more, any organization may harbour bias, may slant or manipulate data. Equally true, the alcohol industry promotes their product, seeking to maintain their multi-billion-dollar market. So, organizations – educational and polit-ical – may misrepresent data, but corporations seek to silence those who slander their golden goose.

I acknowledge, of course, that chemicals don't *make* anyone perform a specific act. Neither booze, nor cocaine, nor metham-phetamines control a person. They don't transform people into chemical robots. A report published by the US Department of Justice states:

> The relationship between alcohol and crime seems to be much more multidimensional. Drinking alcohol (as a single factor) does not cause a person to commit a crime. Additional factors – such as sleep deprivation, a history of alcoholism, psycho-logical disorders, and physical conditions such as temporal lobe dysfunction or hypoglycemia – can play an important role. Any one of these factors in combination with alcohol can affect a person's thinking or response to a situation or opportunity that may lead to a crime being committed. As another group of researchers put it:
>
> 'Causal effects come essentially in the form of an alcohol-person-situation interaction. That is, alcohol consumption increases the probability of violent behavior only for some persons in some situations.'[2]

Undeniably, biological, cultural and individual factors – like choice – play a role in the causal chain resulting in socially detrimental behaviour. The statement above, however, does not tell us anything new or enlightening. We all knew neither alcohol nor drugs change us into robots.

Nonetheless, these chemicals foster socially toxic behaviours and corrosive cultures. They nurture a state of affairs that stains society, ravages families and retards humanity's progress.

Second-hand booze

Every North American recognizes the damage of '*second-hand smoke*'. However, we do not – or will not – admit the harm of '*second-hand booze*'.

Second-hand smoke injures non-smokers. Second-hand booze, therefore, refers to the destructive impact alcohol has on the rest of society. The cost incurred from second-hand booze – I believe – trumps second-hand smoke. The World Health Organization summarizes my concern:

> Alcohol is a psychoactive substance with dependence-producing properties that has been widely used in many cultures for centuries. The harmful use of alcohol causes a large disease, social and economic burden in societies.[3]

Second-hand pickpockets: Economic costs

It is impossible to monetize social, emotional and psychological suffering, and sadly, for some people monetary cost represents the only cost. Regardless, it's upsetting to pay for other people's alcohol use – and the amount is staggering and scandalous.

The National Institute on Alcohol Abuse and Alcoholism, a component of the US National Institutes of Health (NIH), reported in 1998 that:

the economic cost of alcohol and drug abuse was $246 billion in 1992, the most recent year for which sufficient data were available. This estimate represents $965 for every man, woman, and child living in the United States in 1992. The new study reports that alcohol abuse and alcoholism generated about 60 percent of the estimated costs ($148 billion), while drug abuse and dependence accounted for the remaining 40 percent ($98 billion).

'This study confirms the enormous damage done to society by alcohol and drug-related problems,' said NIAAA Director Enoch Gordis, M.D. 'The magnitude of these costs underscores the need to find better ways to prevent and treat these disorders . . .'

'Much of the economic burden of alcohol and drug problems falls on the population that does not abuse alcohol and drugs,' said study author Henrick Harwood and his colleagues at The Lewin Group . . .

Because population increases and inflation have increased the costs further since 1992, the study authors also projected the costs for alcohol and drug abuse for 1995. By adjusting the 1992 estimates for population growth and inflation, they estimated that the 1995 costs to society were $276 billion.[4]

In 1992, the US paid $246 billion, with alcohol causing 60% of that cost: $148 billion. So, booze caused the bulk of the burden, more than all other drugs combined. Understandably, the Institute's director used the phrase 'enormous damage'. Further, note that the cost 'falls on the population that does not abuse alcohol and drugs' and the price increases yearly. Imagine the cost in the 21st century. Imagine, further, this cost considered over a decade: $2.46 trillion.

Numbers this high often cease to make sense. Without a way to gauge them, they neither settle in the mind nor touch the heart. In order to help, consider the $276 billion bill compared to a country's GDP. GDP is the total market value of all final goods and services produced in a country in a given year.

According to the World Bank, the amount of $276 billion exceeds the 2015 GDP of each of the following countries: Pakistan, Chile, Finland, Portugal, Bangladesh, Greece, Vietnam, Peru, Czech Republic, Kazakhstan, Iraq, Romania, New Zealand, Algeria, Qatar, Hungary, Kuwait, Puerto Rico, Angola, Morocco, Ecuador – and 134 other countries![5]

The countries that came under the $300 billion mark were:

+ Israel with over $299 billion
+ Malaysia with over $296 billion
+ Denmark with over $295 billion
+ Singapore and Philippines with over $292 billion
+ Colombia with over $292 billion
+ Ireland with over $283 billion.[6]

To be clear, according to the NIH, the US spent more money on alcohol and drug abuse in 1995 than 150 countries individually would make in a whole year.

If GDP seems too emotionally distant, let's consider the World Food Programme (WFP), the food assistance branch of the United Nations:

Assisting 80 million people in around 80 countries each year, the World Food Programme (WFP) is the leading humanitarian organization fighting hunger worldwide, delivering food assistance in emergencies and working with communities to improve nutrition and build resilience . . .

On any given day, WFP has 20 ships, 70 planes and 5,000 trucks on the move, delivering food and other assistance to those in most need. Every year, we distribute approximately

12.6 billion rations at an estimated average cost per ration of US$ 0.31.[7]

The 2016 budget of the World Food Programme was just shy of $6 billion.[8] Or maybe we could look at the United Nations Children's Fund (UNICEF). In 2015, UNICEF spent US $5.1 billion.[9] This money was spent on:

- supplying 25.5 million people with safe drinking water;
- giving 23 million measles vaccinations to children between six months and 15 years of age;
- providing 7.5 million children aged 3 to 18 with access to formal or non-formal basic education;
- treating two million children aged six months to 59 months for severe acute malnutrition; and
- providing psychosocial support to 3.1 million children.[10]

If we move to health, we can examine the World Health Organization (WHO), whose 2016–2017 budget amounted to US$4.4 billion.[11]

If science proves more inspiring, what is the operating cost of the National Aeronautics and Space Administration (NASA)? According to its website, its 2018 budget proposal was $19 billion. Or we could look at the European Organization for Nuclear Research (CERN). Its 2015 budget (in US currency) was roughly $1.1 billion.[12]

These five institutions – WFP, WHO, NASA, CERN, UNICEF – both scientific and humanitarian, spent a rough total of US$35.4 billion. So, without drug and alcohol abuse, the US alone could increase funding to these institutions *eight-fold*. This thought terrifies me. And yet, the story grows darker, because that was the US alone.

Let us examine a more recent study: *Alcohol in Europe: A*

Public Health Perspective (2006) – a report for the European Commission from the UK Institute of Alcohol Studies:

> Alcohol places a significant burden on several aspects of human life in Europe, which can broadly be described as 'health harms' and 'social harms'.
>
> Seven million adults report being in fights when drinking over the past year and . . . the economic cost of alcohol-attributable crime has been estimated to be €33bn in the EU for 2003. This cost is split between police, courts and prisons (€15bn), crime prevention expenditure and insurance administration (€12bn) and property damage (€6bn). Property damage due to drink-driving has also been estimated at €10bn, while the intangible cost of the physical and psychological effects of crime has been valued at €9bn–€37bn.
>
> An estimated 23 million Europeans are dependent on alcohol in any one year, with the pain and suffering this causes for family members leading to an estimated intangible impact of €68bn.[13]

Everything tallies up: we have seven million violent offences due to drinking, and a whopping total of €43 billion in tangible costs. The study does not, however, include costs related to health, mental health, etc. This represents only 'alcohol-attributable crime'. The estimated *intangible* cost ranges from €77 billion to a possible €105 billion. Of course, it's difficult to calculate 'intangible impact'. How do you monetize the sorrow of watching your child battle with addiction? What is the financial cost of feeling unsafe in your neighbourhood? What price do we put on losing your child to a drunken accident? How much money would you pay to restore the shattered trust of abuse victims? How do you monetize the fallout of seven million assaults per year? We cannot ignore these other costs; simply,

I find it odd (a better word might be 'bizarre') to assign them dollar signs.

Across the Atlantic, the US Department of Justice reports a nearly $60,000,000,000 price tag for underage drinking. You read that correctly: $60 billion. Please note this represents only 'underage' drinking:

> The cost of underage drinking to the US economy alone was estimated at nearly US $58.4 billion in 1994. This figure includes costs of youth involvement in motor vehicle crashes (US$18.2 billion) and violent crime ($35.9 billion), as well as burns, drownings, suicides and alcohol poisonings.[14]

Moving north to Canada – my homeland – the picture remains bleak. The Canadian Centre on Substance Abuse, in 2014, relayed this data:

> The most recent comprehensive cost study, conducted in 2002, estimated the total cost of alcohol-related harm to Canadians to be $14.6 billion per year. This figure includes the following annual costs:
> 1. $7.1 billion in lost productivity due to disability and premature death;
> 2. $3.3 billion for direct health care costs;
> 3. $3.1 billion for direct enforcement costs.[15]

In 2002, the last year for which cost data are available, 30.4% of all police-recorded criminal offences in Canada were attributable to alcohol, which translates to 761,638 police incidents. In total, the policing costs attributable to alcohol were estimated at $1.89 billion that year.

Also in 2002, an estimated 35.8% of all criminal court cases were attributable to alcohol, which translates to 133,120 cases that year. Based on these findings, alcohol-attributable court costs were an estimated $513 million.

... The estimated correctional costs of alcohol-attributable offences were $660.4 million in 2002, with adult corrections making up $502.2 million and youth corrections costing $158.2 million.

In total, enforcement costs (policing, courts and corrections) attributable to alcohol were $3.1 billion in 2002.[16]

Let's remember that Canada has a population of only 36 million. Further, these reports ignore the cost of addiction treatment, family counselling, health and mental health, etc. We see only 'policing, courts and corrections'. And these statistics relate only to alcohol, not cocaine, methamphetamines or other drugs.

Second-hand harm – The devil is in the data

Does alcohol harm society? Of course it does; we all know this. Statistics, however, touch not the heart. Yet from the numerical thicket, the haunted eyes of alcohol's victims peer out. We must, therefore, strain to feel the pain behind the dollar signs, the sorrow obscured by numbers – statistics conceal broken hearts and muddled minds.

Despite finding such research conceptually unnecessary (and emotionally impotent), I push on.

The UK Government's Home Office states:

Alcohol is frequently involved in violent offences; victims believed the offender to be under the influence in 44 per cent of incidents of violent offences. It is estimated that alcohol-related crime costs the economy of England and Wales between £8 billion and £13 billion per year (Home Office, 2010). Research has consistently shown links between crime and disorder, 'binge' drinking and the nighttime economy.[17]

In 2012, British Prime Minister David Cameron spoke frankly about binge drinking:

> Binge drinking isn't some fringe issue, it accounts for half of all alcohol consumed in this country. The crime and violence it causes drains resources in our hospitals, generates mayhem on our streets and spreads fear in our communities.[18]

This expression of concern introduces *The Government's Alcohol Strategy*. On the next page, it states:

> A combination of irresponsibility, ignorance and poor habits – whether by individuals, parents or businesses – led to almost 1 million alcohol-related violent crimes and 1.2 million alcohol-related hospital admissions in 2010/11 alone . . . Society is paying the costs – alcohol-related harm is now estimated to cost society £21 billion annually.[19]

And it continues:

> Communities should not have to tolerate alcohol-related crime and disorder. Almost a quarter (24%) of the public think that drunk or rowdy behaviour is a problem in their local area.[20]

The UK reports alcohol 'draining resources', spreading fear, leading to 1.2 million alcohol-related hospital admissions' and '1 million violent crimes'. Would an intellectually and morally enlightened culture tolerate – let alone celebrate – such a socially ruinous chemical? Once again, if we learned that eating parmesan cheese caused this level of damage, would we (honestly) try to justify our fettuccini alfredo? I don't think so.

To dwell for a time in Britain, the Institute for Alcohol

Studies published a document in 2006 entitled *Alcohol in Europe: A Public Health Perspective*:

> Although the use of alcohol brings with it a number of pleas-
> ures, alcohol increases the risk of a wide range of social harms,
> generally in a dose dependent manner – i.e. the higher the alco-
> hol consumption, the greater the risk . . . Generally the higher
> the level of alcohol consumption, the more serious is the crime
> or injury. The volume of alcohol consumption, the frequency
> of drinking and the frequency and volume of episodic heavy
> drinking all independently increase the risk of violence . . .[21]

> A large number of studies have demonstrated a significantly
> increased risk of involvement in violence among heavy drink-
> ers, who are also more likely to be the recipients of violence.[22]

Crossing the Atlantic, Canada repeats the story. The Canadian
Centre on Substance Abuse (CCSA) claimed in April 2002:

> Alcohol-dependent federal inmates were much more likely to
> have committed a violent crime than were drug-dependent
> inmates, while drug-dependent inmates were more likely to
> have committed a gainful crime.
>   Using this method, the proportion of crimes committed
> by federal and provincial inmates that are attributed to the
> use of alcohol and/or illicit drugs in Canada was estimated
> as being between 40% and 50%. Between 10% and 15% are
> attributed to illicit drugs only, between 15% and 20% are
> attributed to alcohol only, and 10% to 20% are attributed to
> both alcohol and illicit drugs.[23]

Drug-dependent inmates commit 'gainful crime', whereas alcohol generates more violent crime – without gain. Cached out

in common language, drug addicts want money to feed their habit but alcohol generates random violence – not the kind of chemical you want coursing through your country's arteries. The CCSA report continues:

> Among the federal inmates, approximately one half (49%) of violent crimes such as homicide, attempted murder and assault were attributed to alcohol and/or illicit drugs (5% drugs only, 28% alcohol only and 16% drugs and alcohol combined). Similarly, one half (50%) of gainful crimes such as theft, break and enter and robbery were attributed to alcohol and/or illicit drugs (20% drugs only, 11% alcohol only and 19% drugs and alcohol combined) . . . The proportion of other crimes (not included in the violent, gainful and drug crime categories) that were attributed to alcohol or illicit drugs was estimated at 54% (6% drugs only, 35% alcohol only and 14% alcohol and illicit drugs).[24]

The costs of second-hand booze cannot be denied: alcohol harms, and not only the user. These costs range from spousal abuse, financial loss from addiction, depreciated emotional and intellectual interactions (weakened hearts and minds), and increased social fear. This last point merits a moment's attention.

The phrase 'second-hand booze' came to me while discussing Canada's anti-smoking legislation. I expressed how I deplored the similar effects of alcohol. My friends were surprised.

To be candid: I fought addiction for years. Even worse, I also fought people. In my youth, I participated in numerous street fights. I grew up in an aggressive city, spent a lot of time in bars, clubs and pubs and have no illusions about most male patrons' psychological state. I also have no illusions regarding the damage I inflicted on others; I can never erase the images, nor apologize enough for the sorrow I caused.

In later years, I taught martial arts. In self-defence classes, I imparted environmental awareness: know the potential threats in your surroundings. My first question was always, 'Should you be here?' If you get into a confrontation, ask if you knew you were in a violent setting. If so, you had a more effective strategy than martial arts – don't go to those places. My job was to keep people safe, to avoid injury from violence. How could I ignore situational factors?

Often, I asked students to imagine they possess an invisible, odourless gas that makes people completely honest. 'Pump it into any club on a Friday night,' I'd say, 'walk in and yell out, "Raise your hand if you're looking for a fight tonight, or wouldn't mind getting into one?"'

I guarantee fists would shoot into the air. I know this because many former friends would have raised their hands. Depressingly, I would have too.

We've become numb to this reality. When you smoke cigarettes, you're desensitized to the dreadful smell. Similarly, immersed in alcohol-chemical culture, you live behind the veil of normalcy, unaware of the cultural stench.

The UK Institute for Alcohol Studies acknowledges this facet of club culture:

> Although a few incidents that occur in bars involve interpersonal conflict between friends or couples that might have occurred in another setting, almost all incidents of aggression that occur in bars are unplanned, emerge from the social interaction in the bar and often involve strangers.[25]

In Finland, Germany, Norway, Poland and the UK, assault associations seem higher than those for robbery and sexual crimes, although the range of results is also greater and more spread out between victim and offender drinking. Vandalism also shows a strong association with alcohol where data is available (Belgium, Estonia, Latvia and Norway), as does theft in a number of countries. The alcohol-crime link for all of these is stronger for drinking to intoxication – in the UK, for example, 24% of all violent offences are committed by 18-24 year old binge-drinkers, compared to 16% for other regular drinkers and 5% by occasional – or non-drinkers of the same age.[26]

StatsCan – the Canadian Government's central statistics office – published a report in 2005, *Exploring Crime Patterns in Canada*. In the section 'Alcohol and drug consumption' they report:

An established body of research consistently points to the co-occurrence of alcohol or drugs and crime in a substantial proportion of cases. For example:

* A recent Canadian study found that between 40% and 50% of crimes were related to alcohol or drugs, because of intoxication at the time, alcohol or drug dependency, or having committed the crime to obtain drugs or alcohol.
* Drugs or alcohol played a role in the criminal activity of 40% of women in Canadian prisons, while half were under the influence of drugs or alcohol when they committed their current offence.[27]

Exploring the statistical correlation between drug and alcohol use and crime rates, StatsCan reported:

At the macro-level, an association has been established between robbery rates and heroin use. Chilvers and Weatherburn (2003) estimate that each 10% increase in the annual number of dependent heroin users in one state in Australia predicts a 6% increase in the robbery rate. Cook and Moore

(1993) estimate that a hypothetical 10% increase in per capita alcohol consumption in the United States would result in a 6.5% rise in sexual assault, a 1% rise in homicide, a 6% increase in assault and a 9% increase in robbery. Field (1990) also found that variations in beer consumption in the UK were significantly related to rates of violent crime.[28]

The World Health Organization found in 2009 that:

Injuries – both unintentional and intentional – account for more than a third of the burden of disease attributable to alcohol consumption. These include injuries from road traffic crashes, burns, poisoning, falls and drowning as well as violence against oneself or others.[29]

How do you summarize such statistics? More importantly, how do you ignore them?

As the UK Institute for Alcohol Studies stated, 'alcohol increases the risk of a wide range of social harms, generally in a dose dependent manner'.

In the previous section, we examined the cost alcohol inflicts on society, draining resources from socially uplifting goals, resources drowned in a bottle of booze. Yet once again, we can't monetize losing a child to addiction, being beaten on the street, the loss of a loved one to drunk driving. If we can't calculate these losses, how can we possibly compute mislaid potential, the impact of clouded minds, or lost productivity? I lament what would or could have otherwise been.

Before we enter the next section, I want to warn of danger, a danger that comes with reading statistics like these. Our eyes can glaze over, our mind begin to skip past the real people behind the numbers – our hearts can become numb. Please, bear with me, hold your heart open, it's too easy to become distant, numb or callous. We need to support each other as we confront humanity's sorrow. It's the only way we can stop it.

Second-hand booze and the little ones

We shelter coworkers from second-hand smoke. We frown on the mother or father who smokes in the car or in the home. But we allow children, innocent and defenceless individuals, to be exposed to second-hand booze.

We can't gauge the impact on children from a sibling or parent's death, the loss of family income due to chemical dependency, nor the kindnesses stripped from their lives by chemical crutches. The damage, however, ranges far wider. The World Health Organization states:

> The harmful use of alcohol is one of the main risk factors to health. It is responsible each year for about 2.3 million premature deaths worldwide . . . The impact of alcohol-related injuries affects not only those who are intoxicated at the time of injury occurrence, but also those who fall victim to their behavior.
>
> These include the pedestrian or cyclist knocked over by a drunk driver or the woman or children beaten by a drunk husband or father.[30]

The Canadian Statistics Office claims that:

> Rates of spousal violence are higher and injuries more severe in relationships with heavy drinkers. Women victims are more likely than men to say violent partners were drinking at the time of the violent incident.[31]

Violence against women directly affects children. This holds true even when the mother has not yet given birth. Remove the offender, restrain the offence, and the psychological effects of domestic violence (or street fights) do not end. They ripple throughout lives, infecting future relationships, creating fear long after the events. Worse, the tragedies are reincarnated, generation after generation. As a martial arts teacher, I've seen residual fear from abuse many times, and decades after the event.

Studies from the United Kingdom and Ireland indicate that one-third of intimate partner violence occurs when the perpetrator is using alcohol:

> There is an overall relationship between greater alcohol use and criminal and domestic violence, with particularly strong evidence from studies of domestic and sexual violence.[32]

The Institute for Alcohol Studies understands well the impact of second-hand booze:

> Many of the harms caused by alcohol are borne by people other than the drinker responsible. This includes 60,000 underweight births, as well as 16% of child abuse/neglect and 5-9 million children living in families adversely affected by alcohol. Alcohol also affects other adults, including an estimated 10,000 deaths in drink-driving accidents for people other than the drink-driver, with a substantial share of alcohol-attributable crime also likely to occur to others.[33]

Even 500,000 children living 'in families adversely affected by alcohol' is uncivilized; ten times that amount, barbaric. Also, keep in mind that 10,000 drunk-driving deaths means 10,000 mothers who lost their child, 10,000 fathers, thousands more brothers, sisters, aunts, uncles, grandparents – whole social networks violently torn. And yet, this holds true for families battling with addiction. I have lost friends to drugs, and lost the minds of friends to alcohol – and not only on a weekly basis. Some never return, others never flower.

The World Health Organization's 2011 *Global Status Report: Alcohol and Young People* speaks of the effect on youth – the future of civilization:

> Drinking by parents may also harm family life, leading to a variety of deleterious effects on young people. In the European Union alone, a collaborative report from WHO's European Regional Office estimated that 4.5 million young people lived in families adversely affected by alcohol (European Commission 1998). Problems for the young people in such homes may include instability or collapse of marriages and family structures, increased risk of physical or sexual abuse, neglect, and strain on family finances. Such family problems may in turn put young people at greater risk of developing anti-social behaviours, emotional problems and problems in the school environment.[34]

The Substance Abuse and Mental Health Services Administration (SAMHSA), an agency of the US Department of Health and Human Services, found that

> as many as 80 percent of child abuse cases are associated with the use of alcohol and other drugs, and the link between child abuse and other forms of domestic violence is well established
> . . .
>
> Other evidence of the connection between substance abuse and family violence includes the following data:
> * About 40 percent of children from violent homes believe that their fathers had a drinking problem and that they were more abusive when drinking.
> * Childhood physical abuse is associated with later

substance abuse by youth.

- Fifty percent of batterers are believed to have had 'addiction' problems.
- Teachers have reported a need for protective services three times more often for children who are being raised by someone with an addiction than for other children.
- Alcoholic women are more likely to report a history of childhood physical and emotional abuse than are nonalcoholic women.[35]

According to the WHO *Alcohol Fact Sheet* released in 2011: 'Alcohol is associated with many serious social and developmental issues, including violence, child neglect and abuse, and absenteeism in the workplace.'[36]

A final plea

Consider what we've surveyed. Contrast it with the Temple of the Heart: humanity's empathic and altruistic capacity. Shouldn't we cease this injurious social tradition? No doubt, one person cannot undo all this harm, but in aggregate it is the only act that ever will; societies are composed of individuals.

Let's review a small fraction of the data. Assume, further, that the stats are accurate. Imagine: your renunciation of chemical pastimes could:

1. Save the US $27.6 billion per year, with a further $5.8 billion per year in costs related to underage drinking.
2. Save the EU €3.3 billion per year in alcohol-attributable crime and save €1 billion from drunk-driving property damage.
3. End the alcohol dependency of 2.3 million Europeans.
4. Save the Canadian people $1.5 billion dollars yearly from disability, death, healthcare costs and law enforcement caused by alcohol.

5. Save England and Wales £800 million to £1.3 billion per year in alcohol-related crime.
6. Stop 100,000 alcohol-related violent crimes and 120,000 alcohol-related hospital admissions in the UK alone.
7. Stop 76,000 alcohol-induced criminal acts in Canada next year.
8. Prevent 230,000 premature deaths worldwide next year.
9. End alcohol's adverse effects in the lives of 500,000–900,000 European children.

These stats represent a fraction of what we've examined. As well, this fraction is just a fraction of global damage. Our data came from the EU, the UK, the US and Canada. We never examined Russia, South America, the Middle East, or even one Asian country.

Let's recall that we assume that neither you nor I *need* alcohol. We live free of chemical dependence. We need, therefore, only a 'good enough' reason to stop using it. Now, with the nine points above, do we have sufficient evidence to decide society would be happier, healthier, and more harmonious without alcohol? Do we have – in light of the Temple of the Heart – sufficient reason to denounce this drug? I sincerely hope so. If not, are we nearing a sufficient level of harm? What level of societal damage *would* warrant a denunciation of alcohol? Or, has the bar been set impossibly high?

The data is, however, deceptive. It is deceptive because I distorted the statistics in the nine points above. I apologize, for I have played a trick on you. In my ploy, I relied on the mental static caused by statistics, how they fade quickly for most readers. Look again at the original statistics above; I reduced them all by a full 90%. The actual numbers are 10 times higher.

1. It was not $27.6 billion in costs to the US – it was $276 billion.
2. The EU doesn't spend €3.3 billion on alcohol-attributable crime – it's €33 billion.
3. England and Wales don't have £800 million or £1.3 billion yearly in booze-crime – it's £8 billion to £13 billion.
4. There aren't 2.3 million alcohol-dependent Europeans; it's 23 million.
5. Alcohol didn't cost Canada $1.5 billion; they spent $14.6 billion.
6. There weren't 100,000 alcohol-related crimes in the UK – it was 1 million.
7. Canada – with a population of 36 million – actually had 761,638 police incidents due to alcohol, not 76,000.
8. Globally, 2.3 million premature deaths will occur next year from this chemical, not 230,000.
9. And finally, it is 5-9 million European children adversely affected, not 500 to 900 thousand.

I hope you understand my motivation for the momentary deceit, and I hope you'll forgive me for doing so. Yet if the nine points above offer enough reason to denounce chemical crutches, then 10 times the damage gives 10 times the rationale. And if the 10% cannot move the heart, maybe the other 90% will. And if you notice the movement isn't commensurate with the damage, you'll understand why I often find statistics point-less; they rarely affect us emotionally.

Yet, if still the heart remains motionless, one could *now* add all of Asia, Russia, the Balkans, South and Central America, Australia, the Pacific Islands, etc. And if not from this, then what would it take?

As cited earlier from the World Health Organization:

Alcohol is a psychoactive substance with dependence-produc-ing properties that has been widely used in many cultures for centuries. The harmful use of alcohol causes a large disease, social and economic burden in societies.[37]

I end this section with two quotations from the WHO *Global Status Report on Alcohol and Health*:

The harmful use of alcohol is a worldwide problem result-ing in millions of deaths, including hundreds of thousands of young lives lost. It is not only a causal factor in many diseases, but also a precursor to injury and violence. Furthermore, its negative impacts can spread throughout a community or a country, and beyond, by influencing levels and patterns of alcohol consumption across borders.[38]

The impact of alcohol consumption reaches deep into society. Alcohol consumption causes harm far beyond the physical and psychological health of the drinker. It also causes harm to the well-being and health of others. Some social harm to the drinker is implied in the health conditions already examined in this report. Diseases and injuries, for instance, have social implications, including medical costs, which are borne by governments, negative effects on productivity, and financial and psychological burdens on families. Examples of harm caused to others includes prenatal conditions caused by a mother's drinking and injuries from violence caused by an intoxicated assailant. The scope of such social harm stretches beyond these examples. In Australia, a country of 21 million, more than 10 million people have been negatively impacted in some way by a stranger's drinking.[39]

Alcohol injures the user; second-hand booze damages others

– physically, economically, emotionally and psychologically. Second-hand smoke, while repulsive, pales in comparison to the horrid hazards of second-hand booze.

The expected surprise

The data on the harmful effects of drugs and alcohol swamp the psyche. Naturally, numbness ensues. Yet evidence of social toxicity should not shock us. Rather, it's an expected surprise. Expected, because we knew these substances cause damage; surprising, however, because of the severity. The magnitude could crush a tender heart, or make it recoil into denial.

As I've said, I don't think anyone genuinely believes booze to be beneficial; at best, they think it's 'not *that* bad'. We know drugs are detrimental. Yet, we decide they're *acceptably* damaging. However, we veil the consequences of chemical *fun,* try to untangle ourselves from the cognitive dissonance caused by our *pastimes.* Littering – we tell ourselves – is acceptable because many people litter more than we do.

Why do we muffle the sound of suffering? Why shy away from injustice? Sadly, we can often prefer numbness to the pain of reality.

Consider: thousands of children die daily from lack of food, cheap medicine and clean water, but our discomfort is rare. If *this* is so, how could spousal and parental abuse, fetal alcohol syndrome, suicide, assault, rape, damaged livers, emotional distress, cancer, low self-esteem and mental health issues stir our hearts?

How *could* such things alarm us when our current global order, like a ravenous beast, feasts on millions each year? Alcohol's havoc finds no foothold in a heart aware that, at this moment, children hoist automatic weapons for war instead of pens for school; climb trees as snipers instead of as explorers;

practise killing instead of multiplication tables. The negative effects of drugs don't register, because we know little girls learn the sex trade instead of the violin, enter sweatshops instead of playgrounds, make shoes instead of make-believe.

This causes me great sorrow; yet numbness still claims the lion's share of my heart. I study the damage these chemicals inflict on cities, nations and families. I don't drink or do drugs, but I often don't (or won't) acknowledge the damage. How much greater the aversion must be for a drug or alcohol *user*.

Often, we avoid investigation because moral responsibility weighs heavily. And we can't face our failure to change. There is beauty in this; certainly, it would be *far* more shameful to feel no remorse at all. Yet we must mature further and accept the ramifications of our decisions on those around us.

While driving, you hear on the radio that passengers are trapped in a burning car. You shake your head, saddened momentarily by their suffering. You feel justified, however, as you continue driving to work, instead of rushing to help. However, if you were present you might feel differently.

Standing at an intersection, you see a family driving along, the parents smiling as children laugh in the back seats. Then, a truck plows into the side of their minivan. It spins violently, broken glass showering onlookers. An explosive sound splits the air as the van slams into a light post. Instantly, fire bursts from the engine, its flames licking the windshield. You hear a scream. You smell the smoke and gasoline . . . and walk away, wondering if there is a coffee shop nearby.

If we witness suffering and refuse to alter our actions, the ensuing psychological dissonance will prove unbearable. Thus, we remove the source of moral discomfort, and remain numb. We ignore reality to maintain our minds.

It's as if your mom kept calling you, hoping for a chat. But you never pick up. Days, weeks and months go by, and your shame grows. She still calls once or twice a week, leaving messages, expressing her love, her voice sad with the pain of neglect. Your guilt increases with each passing day. So you finally bite the bullet, steel yourself for action, call your mobile provider and cancel your number. There – problem solved. Instead of climbing the mount of responsibility, you slide downslope and delete the source of discomfort.

Strangely, this truly does reveal our tenderness, our compassion. Paradoxically, we choose to remain numb and ignorant *because* we care. We avoid confronting reality because it hurts to witness misery. Our discomfort is manifested when we observe anguish – the starving child, the sex trade worker, the child soldier, the home broken by booze – because we are moral beings. I do not hope for self-deprecation, but rather honesty, courage and then resolve. It is to this reality that we must turn, instead of turning away.

A touch too quickly

The most common response to these drugs' destruction is the rapid reply: 'Well, these people are reckless. They're drunks! I'm not like that. I drink responsibly.'

I made this reply when I drank. It's a natural reaction. Yet, to be frank, the retort, 'But I don't do *that!*' comes a tad too quickly.

After seeing alcohol's poisonous effects, I wish a moment of silence would follow, instead of a reactionary retort. Surely, I admire those who avoid destructive behaviour, but the comeback acknowledges people's terrible irresponsibility with these chemicals. Still, despite the lack of tact, the 'responsible drinker' point demands proper consideration.

The glory of the heart: The gift of sacrifice

Religions call us to sacrifice for humanity, a sacrifice that, by definition, involves discomfort, even pain. The steep and stony path to nobility demands we forgo our own delight for the needs of others. The Temple of the Heart pulsates with this hymn. And Bahá'u'lláh sings this anthem to all humankind:

> Do not busy yourselves in your own concerns; let your thoughts be fixed upon that which will rehabilitate the fortunes of mankind and sanctify the hearts and souls of men.[40]

Bahá'u'lláh – as with all Manifestations of God – asks that we choose others before ourselves. This quality of character generates our admiration for figures like Mother Teresa, Nelson Mandela, Martin Luther King Jr. and Mahatma Gandhi. These social activist icons enchant us because they forgo their comfort – even their lives, be they short or long – for humankind. Conversely, this quality's absence is leading our world into ruin.

A narrative interlude: Jamen and the homeless heart

My friend Jamen and I walked through the streets of Vancouver, oblivious to the world around us. Discussions on religion, society and the meaning of life consumed our attention. You see, my new friend followed a peculiar Middle Eastern religion I had only recently heard of – the Bahá'í Faith. I found the dialogues intriguing, full of new perspectives. Suddenly, the topic of alcohol arose.

Surprised to hear Jamen didn't drink, I asked why. He responded with a predictable litany of alcohol's social detriments. My reliable retort prepared to pounce. He finished, and I fired: 'But Jamen, I don't have those problems. Yeah, sure booze causes some harm, but I don't drink all day. I don't hit my girl-friend, or my kids. I don't have a problem with my job. I drink and don't go overboard. I drink responsibly. Not everyone who drinks is an idiot. So, why should *I* quit drinking?'

I was sure the conversation was now over. Slowing down, Jamen spoke quietly, 'I agree. I don't have those problems, and maybe you don't either. But, you know why I don't drink, Rob?'

Jamen stopped and pointed across the street. And there, as if on cosmic cue, lay a husk of a man, curled up in the doorway, his clothes caked with dirt, pants tattered, wrapped in a ripped and stained jacket. And cuddled in his arms, tucked up under his chin, was a bottle of wine, swaddled in the stained folds of a brown paper bag – a manifest cliché.

'I don't drink for *him*,' Jamen said sadly. 'I don't care if I don't have a problem,' he continued, 'I care that he does. If I can forgo something I don't *need* to free the world from *that*, I'll do it.'

My gift to you

Jamen's reply was, in principle, 'So what if you don't have a problem? It leads people down dark paths, injures our broth-ers and sisters, destroying bodies, hearts and minds. So, for the sake of others, for community, for the progress of civilization, give it up. And if you don't need it, why not stop for them?' He sacrificed his desires for the needs of the world, a gift that would ennoble society, something it sorely needs.

Naturally, in a tremendously individualistic society, Jamen's reply sounds peculiar. The belief that individual interests reign supreme is comfortably hidden behind the veil of normalcy, its ascendancy unchallenged, its influence undetected.

The moral and emotional tidiness of this view is impres-sive. We can deny responsibility for the ripple effects of our thoughts, our words, our deeds. Yet rather than a hammered out philosophical position, people often use this belief to free themselves from the *fetters* of responsibility, the *burden* of duty, the *weight* of accountability, and any possibility of shame. But nobility follows a different path. Bahá'u'lláh proclaims:

> Be generous in prosperity, and thankful in adversity. Be worthy of the trust of thy neighbor, and look upon him with a bright and friendly face. Be a treasure to the poor, an admonisher to the rich, an answerer of the cry of the needy, a preserver of the sanctity of thy pledge. Be fair in thy judgement, and guarded in thy speech. Be unjust to no man, and show all meekness to all men. Be as a lamp unto them that walk in darkness, a joy to the sorrowful, a sea for the thirsty, a haven for the distressed, an upholder and defender of the victim of oppression. Let integrity and uprightness distinguish all thine acts. Be a home for the stranger, a balm to the suffering, a tower of strength for the fugitive. Be eyes to the blind, and a guiding light unto the feet of the erring. Be an ornament to the countenance of truth, a crown to the brow of fidelity, a pillar of the temple of righteousness, a breath of life to the body of mankind, an ensign of the hosts of justice, a luminary above the horizon of virtue, a dew to the soil of the human heart, an ark on the ocean of knowledge, a sun in the heaven of bounty, a gem on the diadem of wisdom, a shining light in the firmament of thy generation, a fruit upon the tree of humility.[41]

Such qualities will birth a civilization of light and beauty. Valiant acts of strength and sacrifice, of empathy and compassion, free from the fetters of ephemeral desires, will make humanity whole. Even if you don't spread sorrow and violence, consider abstinence for the sake of humanity. And by serving humankind, ennoble your own soul.

Part of me genuinely fears what Bahá'u'lláh's words entail. That part worries what being a 'breath of life to the body of mankind, an ensign of the hosts of justice' requires of me. To be 'a balm to the suffering', a 'lamp unto them that walk in darkness' is a noble goal, inspiring, challenging, and therefore frightening. But the sickly sweetness of my desires (albeit more tangible and immediate) pale in comparison to the joys of an upright character, a clear conscience, and a loving heart.

A little too close to the bone, or 'What would it take?'

Note the stirrings of your heart. If my alcoholic father beat my mother, siblings and me, many could empathize with my abstinence. If a drunk driver killed my parents, more people would sympathize with my sobriety. Had I been abused by an inebriated *so-called* lover, a rapid retort might be stilled. The human heart, confronted by pain with a face, suffering with a name, pauses prior to brushing it off. Charities are well aware of this principle. Therefore, they introduce you to 'Little Jane', 'Young Bobby' or 'Sick Susan'. They know statistics and abstract appeals fail to reach the heart. People find a touchstone in the suffering of an actual person. This is why statistics often fail.

One day, you learn that a coworker doesn't drink. You ask why. In response, she recounts a litany of injuries she suffered due to alcohol. Her parents, both alcoholics, beat her regularly. In adolescence, a drunk driver killed her friend. Later, her uncle died from cirrhosis, alcoholism being a family trait. That year, a group of drunkards hospitalized her, fracturing her jaw, leaving her lying in an alley to die. You're stunned, silent for a time, eyes wide in shock, your first attempts to respond crumble into false starts and stutters.

After composing yourself, you say, 'Did that actually happen to you!?' Your coworker replies, 'Well, no. Not to me. But it *has* happened – and is happening – to others, all the time. So I avoid alcohol for their sake.'

I think this a reasonable point. And I think we should ask ourselves, 'What is it going to take?' How many bodies need to be bruised, how many minds mangled, how many empathetic hearts emaciated before we drop the drink? We can empathize with those we don't know. So let's acknowledge the damage, sacrifice our desires, and say, 'No more' – so sings the Temple of the Heart.

Social activism: 'Little old me' and 'relative gravity'

Many of us (if not all) cannot comprehend how to stop the avalanche of troubles torturing our world. Our feebleness freezes us before we begin. *Why even try? It's hopeless.* Sadly, this thought can work as a welcome excuse, a pseudo-philosophical alibi. It sounds convincing. In the jury of society (at this point in time), the *futility alibi* offers our more brutish side a convincing case against its higher counterpart: the sage, the servant. It's a fantastic deal. You get the illusion of empathy without the responsibility, duty or sacrifice; you get to eradicate guilt – a seductive bargain.

I call this the '*little old me*' response. What can *little old me* do? I'd like to help but, what can *little old me* do. People say their recycling won't heal the world: *What's little old me going to achieve?* They claim a couple of dollars can't alleviate the tidal wave of human misery? So what's the point? *What can little old me do?* Examples are endless.

The idea is understandable, but it is also blind to human history. It ignores the undeniable reality that all great social movements started somewhere, with someone: a *little old* him, a *little old* her. They originated from apparently insignificant acts, by ostensibly unimportant people. Compared to the crushing cultural momentum of the problem, such solutions clearly appeared useless. They weren't.

Slavery didn't end because a whole culture, in an instant, proclaimed it unethical, like some instantaneous and universal enlightenment. Individuals endured intense pressure, fought against overwhelming odds, to accomplish the freedom of millions. Recycling did not descend into the minds of millions who, like the opening surge of a symphony, began at once to recycle in concert. The emancipation of women was not (and is not) a tidal wave created and carried on by the universal and unstoppable forces of physics. *Every* social transfiguration had an origin, an infinitesimal beginning, from which whole cultures were changed; each genesis had its 'Let there be light!' It always happens this way. It must. Cultural transformation demands a revolutionary stance, a stance taken by millions unnamed in our history books, but not a million at a time.

In contemplating social action, a question arises: which battlefront do I fight on? Not an easy question. An ocean of social ills surrounds us, and the choices we make reveal a peculiar quality of our culture. I know people passionate about eliminating the fur trade, dolphin hunting or the killing of seals. Others serve in multi-cultural societies, helping immigrants integrate into society. I know ardent opponents of homelessness. I've had, in short, the blessing of meeting many noble souls, ones willing to sacrifice their time and energy to alleviate suffering. But these same people often look confused when they learn I don't drink. Their confusion, to me, proves how entrenched this chemical pastime is in our culture.

The unquestioning acceptance of drugs, in this case, dawned on me one evening in an explosion of irony. A coworker asked if I would attend a charity event to help homeless people on the downtown east side of Vancouver, an area notorious for substance abuse and prostitution. The proceeds, he said, would go to shelters and addiction houses. He'd rented a hall, and there was to be finger-food and dancing. The majority of proceeds would come, however, from the sale of alcoholic drinks. I was shocked further when he asked if I'd like some Ecstasy to 'liven up' my night. He'd bought a bunch to sell to friends.

I pointed out – too abruptly – the irony of selling booze (and drugs) to help people devastated by booze and drugs. Obviously, he hadn't considered this – his slackened face the telltale sign. Despite my attempts (somewhat tainted now) to praise his intentions, he changed the topic, walked away, and avoided me for the rest of the evening. The party went on as planned.

When (or if) we consider social activism, we ought to assess the various paths of service – which is most important, most needed? I do not proclaim ending drug use the acme of social causes. I feel surprised, however, that people *rarely* consider it even a limping competitor in the race, especially since it's free and requires no sacrifice of time either. In fact, you save money, increase physical well-being, and free up time. Sure, drug and alcohol addiction programmes may be worth supporting, but abstinence? Of course, we're opposed to sweatshops, but to stop buying their products – that's going too far . . .?

Utopian idealism, the law of sacrifice, and bad math

Often, I speak on world unity, the end of poverty, the unity of science and religion, or universal education. When I do, people call me naïve. Understandably, this also occurs when I say our chemical pastimes will end. They call the vision 'utopian', and me, an 'idealist'.

Often, I hear, 'Rob, you're an idealist. It's never going to happen. Be realistic!' To this I reply, 'Why not call me an optimist, and tell me to be pessimistic?' Typically, this causes confusion.

If you propose social progress – and the listener disagrees – you're 'an idealist'. You don't live in the *real* world, your mind clouded by an unreachable, ideal vision of humanity. In contrast, the accuser is a realist – true-to-life about ways of the world. However, if the listener agrees with the goal, believes in the cause, you're 'an optimist' – no longer the naïve idealist. Suddenly, your mind is free, unrestricted by negative and limited perspectives, uninhibited by the ingrained patterns sapping society's life. But why call you an optimist? Why not brand you a head-in-the-clouds idealist?

We are often oblivious to the flipping of terms – idealist/ optimist and realist/pessimist. Frighteningly, this subconscious semantic game allows us to brush off a belief system with a single word. It is, however, not an argument; it's wordplay.

The goal may, however, *appear* unachievable. This is why people commonly call it utopian or idealistic. My equally common reply is, 'So what?' Branding a goal idealistic or utopian is still not an argument.

Ending slavery *appeared* unrealistic, but thank God we did it. Diseases now in the dustbin of history – at least in the West – surely *looked* impossible to eradicate at one point. Yet I'm glad no one listened to detractors. Unifying Europe after two major world wars *sounded* ridiculous – the League of Nations a pipe dream, the United Nations (after the collapse of the former) absurd, but I'm delighted we kept going. Women's suffrage, civil rights for black and coloured people, the right to education, labour relations, a Declaration of Human Rights – all appeared impossible, at some time, to some people. Consequently, when a chemical-free culture is called idealistic, respond: 'So what?' Noble pursuits always *appear* unreachable, distant and hopeless – even to those who eventually get them done.

An important principle stands manifest before us: You don't get a lot for a little. Evolving physically, morally, intellectually and spiritually entails forgoing ingrained attachments, putting aside ephemeral pursuits, subduing the near-constant desire for ease and comfort. Would we honestly expect it to be any other way? The just, the good, the true, the beautiful – they demand sacrifice. Always.

For example, I may long to be a wonderful pianist, but I'll never achieve it without hours of gruelling practice. Many yearn to be Olympic gymnasts; few are willing to bleed for it. Physics is a glorious science, but you will never grasp it without intense discipline. If I wish to be an expert programmer, a skilled mechanic, an adept potter, an accomplished historian, a perceptive doctor, a gifted lawyer – and on and on it goes – I will struggle and sweat, fail and fall, get beat down, then get up and fight again. If we find this principle self-evident, why expect the pattern to change? Why anticipate no sacrifice when morality steps on stage?

Great social change, progress in our communities, breaching new frontiers of physical reality, learning to manage our thoughts and emotions, are exalted goals. Consequently, they demand heroic levels of sacrifice and discipline – qualities causally linked to pain. Yet such toil and pain are irrelevant; they are worth it.

The point and the bottom bar

Remember: we don't *need* alcohol to have fun, to relieve stress, or socialize comfortably. And if we live free of chemical dependence, why drink if it causes widespread suffering? The human heart shows its beauty by forfeiting desires to alleviate misery. Yes, such acts demand a price: sacrifice, discipline and pain. Yet all worthy goals come with costs. To build the Temple of the Heart, and maintain it, we will pay a fee.

The Temple of the Heart is fashioned with love and

compassion, ornamented with sacrifice and discipline, adorned with independence and responsibility. Therefore, casting aside alcohol and drugs honours the beauty of its architecture.

The *bottom bar* is what we ought to concede. If you continue using drugs and alcohol, esteem those who don't. Rather than viewing them with confusion, pity or disdain, admire them. Our culture often scorns those who pay homage at the Temple of the Heart. They need your encouragement.

4

The Temple of the Mind

Animal emblems and inanimate icons

The natural world abounds with emblems of beauty, power and grace. Many creatures embody attributes we long to emulate, qualities that capture our attention and summon our esteem. Certain animals stand as archetypes, symbolizing moral or intellectual attributes down the ages.

Consider the lion, emblematic of power and authority, courage and nobility. This impressive beast adorns countless entryways, flags, coat of arms, shields, banners and tapestries. The ferocious feline has provoked fear and respect in countless cultures, signifying virtues we venerate and qualities we yearn to possess.

The peacock commands a comparable place, standing for beauty, poise, and elegance in culture after culture. We represent it in poems, song, and story, employ it as a paragon of splendour on frieze and fresco, on porticos and paintings across the globe. This is not *merely* a bird; it is a symbol, an emblem.

The eagle also stands as exemplar. This sovereign of the skies subdues the winds, its eyes scanning with incredible precision, its form dignified and noble. No wonder this regal raptor similarly adorns emblems, logos and flags, bags, banners and backpacks. Watching this creature, we understand why so many seek to associate with its qualities.

Interestingly, the distinguishing qualities of these animal archetypes can be few, at times even singular. Deprived of its glorious tail, for example, the peacock loses most of its exemplary beauty. This one feature marks the bird's magnificence.

Other kingdoms also signify iconic qualities. Mineral and plant icons display this near *symbolic singularity*. Imagine a diamond depleted of sparkle, gold deprived of its shimmering hue. They would be *mere* rocks. Picture a rose without its exquisite form. It would no longer be a rose. The iconic stature can be stripped, at times, with the removal of a sole feature. Remove one attribute, and the glory vanishes.

The human emblem

So, what distinguishes humanity? In most areas, we look longingly at kingdom Animalia; we are slower, weaker, less agile and more breakable than the beasts of field, forest and jungle. Yet, do we – like peacock, eagle or gold – possess an exemplary feature, one quality in particular that differentiates us? We surely do. Where do we tower over mineral, plant and animal? One attribute should instantly come to mind – the mind.

This is the Temple of the Mind, and few bounties can surpass what 'Abdu'l-Bahá' calls the 'priceless gift of intelligence':

The Heavenly Father gave the priceless gift of intelligence to man so that he might become a spiritual light, piercing the darkness of materiality, and bringing goodness and truth into the world.[1]

'Abdu'l-Bahá extols science and rationality:

The virtues of humanity are many, but science is the most noble of them all. The distinction which man enjoys above and beyond the station of the animal is due to this paramount virtue. It is a bestowal of God; it is not material; it is divine. Science is an effulgence of the Sun of Reality, the power of investigating and discovering the verities of the universe, the means by which man finds a pathway to God.[2]

The Temple of the Mind gifts us with science, which 'Abdu'l-Bahá praises glowingly:

Science is the first emanation from God toward man. All created beings embody the potentiality of material perfection, but the power of intellectual investigation and scientific acquisition is a higher virtue specialized to man alone . . . God has created or deposited this love of reality in man. The development and progress of a nation is according to the measure and degree of that nation's scientific attainments.[3]

And His homage to intellect continues:

All blessings are divine in origin, but none can be compared with this power of intellectual investigation and research, which is an eternal gift producing fruits of unending delight. Man is ever partaking of these fruits. All other blessings are temporary; this is an everlasting possession. Even sovereignty has its limitations and overthrow; this is a kingship and dominion which none may usurp or destroy. Briefly, it is an eternal blessing and divine bestowal, the supreme gift of God to man. Therefore, you should put forward your most earnest efforts toward the acquisition of science and arts. The greater your attainment, the higher your standard in the divine purpose . . . A scientific man is a true index and representative of humanity, for through processes of inductive reasoning and research he is informed of all that appertains to humanity, its status, conditions and happenings. He studies the human body politic, understands social problems and weaves the web and texture of civilization. In fact, science may be likened to a mirror wherein the infinite forms and images of existing things are revealed and reflected. It is the very foundation of all individual and national development. Without this basis of investigation, development is impossible. Therefore, seek with diligent endeavor the knowledge and attainment of all that lies within the power of this wonderful bestowal.[4]

In summary, God gave us this 'priceless gift of intelligence'. It was, in fact, the 'first emanation from God toward man'. We must honour the 'love of reality' and this 'power of intellectual investigation'. He deposited these within us, and no other blessing 'can be compared with this power of intellectual investigation'. It is a sovereignty without limitations, a dominion 'none may usurp' – the 'supreme gift of God to man'. We find that the 'scientific man is a true index and representative of humanity'.

This Temple towers over the landscape. We must, therefore, grant it appropriate honour. The Bahá'í Writings glorify this essential emblem of humanity; please keep this in mind as we circle the sanctuary of reason: The Temple of the Mind.

Human intellect, like a mighty tree, confers the fruits of civilization. From its branches, we pluck history, political science, law and philosophy. Sociology, anthropology and economics, as well, are delectable harvests of reason. We gather geology, biology and physics from the same branches, bringing forth conceptual and technological wonders. History, art and mathematics ornament and order our worlds with their splendour and precision.

Putting aside higher concepts, human ingenuity produces

marvels we call everyday objects – a table lamp, a cheese grater, a screwdriver, a drill, a dishwasher, a microwave. These creations – born of intellect – are miraculous machines, despite now being commonplace. Whether we look at furniture, philosophy or physics, paleontology, politics or paper clips, the rational mind birthed them. We are – to a high degree – defined by our intellect.

In the Writings of 'Abdu'l-Bahá we find another eulogy to intellect:

> God's greatest gift to man is that of intellect, or understanding.
>
> The understanding is the power by which man acquires his knowledge of the several kingdoms of creation, and of various stages of existence, as well as of much which is invisible . . .
>
> Intellect is, in truth, the most precious gift bestowed upon man by the Divine Bounty. Man alone, among created beings, has this wonderful power . . .
>
> Study the sciences, acquire more and more knowledge. Assuredly one may learn to the end of one's life! Use your knowledge always for the benefit of others; so may war cease on the face of this beautiful earth, and a glorious edifice of peace and concord be raised.[5]

'God's greatest gift' is our 'intellect, or understanding'. He bids us 'study the sciences' until the 'end of one's life', utilizing such knowledge 'for the benefit of others'.

Thus, in the Bahá'í Writings, the mind is our peacock's tail, our glorious eagle's wings, our noble and ferocious feline features. Through it we tower over animals, creating conceptual realms of extreme complexity, fashioning soaring civilizations. Bereft of this gleaming quality, we are dull and dark, lowered to the level of beasts. No wonder then, that Bahá'u'lláh states:

It is inadmissible that man, who hath been endowed with reason, should consume that which stealeth it away. Nay, rather it behoveth him to comport himself in a manner worthy of the human station, and not in accordance with the misdeeds of every heedless and wavering soul.[6]

Bahá'u'lláh prohibits anything that reduces our reasoning powers. This defining human attribute – a most precious gift of God – cannot be cast aside. We neglect our very reality when we blunt our brains. Drugs and alcohol, therefore, remove what makes us truly human.

Why choose to be a peacock shorn of its exquisite tail, a dull opaque diamond, a chunk of grimy gold? Why decide to be a lion bereft of its teeth and claws, a once-proud sovereign now soft and slow? When we willingly deplete our intellects, we become gold shedding our lustre, or diamonds dulling our pristine shimmer – a dismal thought.

A curious quarrel

People rationalize chemical pastimes, and therein lies a sad irony, an irony I missed until long after I stopped using alcohol and drugs. People use rational arguments to justify ingesting chemicals for fun. But those same chemicals handicap – if not incapacitate – the organ of debate: the mind. People use reason, therefore, to justify ingesting a substance that robs them of cogent thought.

I find it all the more disturbing because I did this myself many times; I offered what I thought were cogent arguments to defend my chemical pastimes. I was a peacock using my glorious tail to argue for ripping out my plumage, a diamond using my sparkle to justify dulling my own sheen. I believe, if pondered and meditated upon, this simple point gives sufficient reason to drop the drugs. All the Temple of the Mind could be reduced to this one point.

A tale of tragedy

The day is brilliant. You walk down a forest path, the sun's heat calmed by a breeze wafting through the trees. Coming to a clearing, you pause and listen to the sounds of bees as they flit among the flowers. You breathe in nature's calming aromas. All around you, life bustles and thrives.

Entering the meadow, you hear a sound in the tall grass, a rustling. An animal draws near. The creature is about to cross into view. Finally, you see it, and your breath stops.

The – whatever it is – drags itself onto the path, sort of slithering, its body covered in dirt, gasping for breath. Its frame twitches as it lurches along. You can't make out what it is. Suddenly, you feel ill.

It's an eagle – or once was. Filth obscures its white crown, feathers muddled by dirt and grime. Its beak – used to drag itself – has become dull and cracked. The feathers on its once proud chest are gone, its breast mere scrapes and sores.

What, you wonder, brought this creature so low? What made this sovereign of the skies writhe in the dirt? Its wings must be clipped, broken or damaged. Approaching cautiously, you examine it, search for injury, but find nothing. Its body is too muddled to make anything out. Saddened, you wrap the bird in your jacket, carry it to your car, and transport it to the animal rescue shelter.

Unnerved by the experience, you return each week to check on its progress: no improvements. Months go by. Still, the bird drags itself along by its beak, effacing its former beauty, despite all attempts to aid it. Finally, you express your confusion to the veterinarians at the animal shelter. 'Why can't it fly?' you ask,

'Why won't it – at least – hop around?' The answer crushes you; the eagle *chooses* not to.

You are startled. Why choose to slither through mire and clay, when you could soar? I pose the same question to our culture. As Bahá'u'lláh laments:

> Ye are even as the bird which soareth, with the full force of its mighty wings and with complete and joyous confidence, through the immensity of the heavens, until, impelled to satisfy its hunger, it turneth longingly to the water and clay of the earth below it, and, having been entrapped in the mesh of its desire, findeth itself impotent to resume its flight to the realms whence it came. Powerless to shake off the burden weighing on its sullied wings, that bird, hitherto an inmate of the heavens, is now forced to seek a dwelling-place upon the dust.[7]

The sky is our home. Why do we satisfy ourselves with dirt? Why crawl when we are meant to climb? We must consider this question. The wings of civilization are love and reason. They support the plumage of philanthropy and philosophy, self-sacrifice and science. When we clip them, we plummet.

We call our recreational chemicals mind-altering drugs. But let's drop equivocations and euphemisms; they are – undeniably – mind-depleting drugs. Therefore, our cherished chemical culture is a factory for fashioning flightless eagles.

Your pal Purdy, the confused peacock

My eagle analogy may irritate. Portraying an intoxicated person as an eagle dragging itself through the dirt seems unfair, if not overly harsh. Yet what *are* humanity's defining characteristics? What *would* be our wings? I proposed intellect and virtue

85

– proposals difficult to deny. And in each case, I must remove the defining quality. Would a timid lion, a drab rose, or a dull brittle diamond better express it?

I admit, however, a problem remains with the eagle analogy. People don't self-medicate constantly. Even hardcore drug users have lucid moments. Rather, most people partake occasionally and lead effective and happy lives. An eagle dragging itself through the dirt day after day is unfair. The objection, I imagine, sounds like this: 'Of course, I don't agree with being an alcoholic. But, I don't do that! I drink a glass of wine with dinner or have a couple of beers with friends. And I don't even do *that* every day.'

This was my response for years.

Yet, the slithering eagle analogy doesn't present the problem of constant drug use. The real problem is wanting to at all. Why would you *ever* choose to slither like a snake if you're an eagle? The response 'I only drink once in a while' fails to grasp the argument; hence, why I call this response 'the confused peacock'.

You've had a long day and want to go home and rest. However, you haven't seen your friend Purdy in quite some time, and he's such a remarkable fellow. He is, after all, a talking peacock.

Arriving at his house, you find the door open. You are close friends, so you walk in and call out, 'Hey Purdy!' You hear noises from down the hall. As you get closer, you become concerned. You hear a series of grunts, a cry of pain, followed by an odd elated giggle. Puzzled, you push open the door.

Purdy is standing in the middle of his office. As you enter, he turns. Clasped tightly in his beak is a clump of his tail feathers, more are strewn on the ground. You are stunned.

'Purdy. What are you doing?'

'Oh nothing, just messing around, having some fun,' he replies.

Your unease grows. 'Why are there feathers all over the

ground?' Your eyes flit from the feathered floor to fixate on the bundle in his beak.

'Oh. I was pulling out my tail feathers,' he replies calmly.

Your heart tightens. Your eyes widen. You work hard to control your voice.

'Purdy, *why* would you *do* that? What's wrong with you?'

Purdy pauses, looks confused and then irritated.

'What's the big deal? I don't do it all the time. Besides, they'll grow back!'

Imagine having to offer Purdy reasons why he shouldn't pull out his tail feathers. Imagine further that, when you point out he's destroying his most beautiful feature, he responds, 'It's no problem. They'll grow back.' Would you feel that much better if they grew back the next morning? Would all your concern disappear? I don't think so.

The problem is that *he doesn't see the problem.* Why would he disfigure himself *at all* – let alone his most superb feature? Can he not see how depressing this is?

Wanting to erode your intellectual abilities *at all* is the issue. Purdy's confusion and the reason for my sadness is not primarily a matter of how frequently he tears out his plumage, nor how rapidly they return. For a confused peacock to answer, 'But I only do it once in a while' shows how oblivious he is to his own beauty – like we are.

Wow! Did you see that girl's dress?

Our culture obsesses over physical appearance. This claim shouldn't need justification. Yet even individuals who don't obsess over body image and fashion consider their appearance. We colour-coordinate our attire. I try to. We wear deodorant, cut our hair, brush our teeth, and shave or trim, and that's for a normal outing. We attend to our appearance, seeking to accentuate our beauty, or mask perceived ugliness.

Our culture is preoccupied with grooming. Surely, we've reached excess. Yet ignore appearance completely and you'll *justifiably* attract attention. Would you regularly leave home without touching up your sleep-tousled hair or patting down a cowlick? Would you feel awkward speaking to coworkers with a chunk of food jutting out of your teeth? Imagine being at a dinner party, and gazing in a mirror to find a large snot-ball hanging out of your nostril. Most of us would be slightly embarrassed.

After discovering a large pasta stain on their shirt, how many people would leave the house without changing? After an hour on the treadmill, how many would attend a meeting without deodorant? How many would leave pizza sauce on their face? None, or very nearly none. Yet, how many people will social-ize with eyes glazed, motor skills impaired, confused or garbled words falling from their lips, their train of thought flitting? I assume the answer – in direct contrast to *all* previous ones – is: 'Most people I know.'

Isn't this peculiar? People who are worried about stained clothes, food-filled teeth, their hair out of line or clothes unmatched, may feel at ease walking around drunk. The same people appalled by snot hanging from their nose wouldn't think twice about being incoherent in front of friends or even col-leagues. Why the discrepancy? The answer is simple: *everyone else is doing it.*

I do not delight in crudeness, so I preemptively apologize, therefore, for the next two sentences. I would rather pass gas, smell of body odour, have food wedged in my teeth, or display nasal mucus, than be drunk or stoned in public. I would rather burp out loud during a symphony than interrupt the mind's harmony for the same length of time.

You don't have to agree, but it can't be that odd. Imagine

going to a bar where people eat nasal mucus, or smear their faces with ketchup. If that is odd to you, going to a club where people devour their own intellects (by the pint) should be (at least) similarly bizarre. The mind is more precious than the body, or rather, it should be.

Vindicating vulgarity?

Apologies if I seem repetitive here, but I cannot allow myself to be misunderstood. Therefore, prior to moving on, I want to address my reference to nasal mucus, flatulence, armpit odour, etc. They appear inappropriate, unbecoming. But I hope to affect a perceptual shift in my readers. I want us to see the world differently.

People spill things on themselves – that's mere physics. We miss things in our teeth, get busy and forget our hair – a simple consequence of being human. As well, bodily functions are wholly natural. Our body produces liquids: saliva, urine, nasal mucus, feces, sweat, tears and blood. Our hair falls out, or grows in odd places. Our skin sags, wrinkles and becomes discoloured. In the end, we age, our bodies fail, and we die.

Please consider this deeply: if we deem mishaps or bodily functions unfitting or improper, *this whole book is inappropriate.* Why?

This work discusses practices that I suggest should be far *more* embarrassing or inappropriate than essential biological functions ordained by God. It is, in contrast, unnatural – *unbecoming our dignity* – to ingest mind-depleting chemicals. It is in this light that – speaking of opium – 'Abdu'l-Bahá stated: 'Fortunate are they who never even speak the name of it; then think how wretched is the user.'[8]

If we venerate the mind, the topic of drugs is more inappropriate, more beneath our dignity, than any natural bodily process. We don't find talk of mind-depleting chemicals as unbecoming, because it's commonplace. Please consider honestly; if you grew up in a world where we passed gas publicly, or ate nasal mucus, the mention wouldn't cause giggles, or furrowed brows. It would – sadly – be normal and appropriate.

This is why I chose those analogies; we must relearn what *truly* crude topics are. If properly understood, I didn't suddenly reference inappropriate topics now, in this section; rather, the vulgar and inappropriate topic began on page 1 of this book.

Nevertheless, I apologize for causing any discomfort. Early on, I discussed 'modern blasphemies' and 'judging judgemental people' – topics that may trigger unease. I do this to highlight a cultural tendency: we find *forbidden fruit* enticing. Often, we perceive 'the bad' as tantalizing, 'the naughty,' 'the sinful' as enigmatic, rebellious, and alluring. We're attracted to the 'bad boy' or 'naughty girl'. They're beguiling *because* they're banned. We love our *sinful* pleasures.

Yet, the last thing I want is for us to see alcohol as *bad, naughty* or *sinful* – that's the appeal! We need to recognize chemical pastimes as *sad*, not *bad*. We must awaken from the immature illicit illusion, and see drug use clearly, as timid, disappointing, limiting and unbecoming of our human dignity.

Prohibiting prohibition

I hope I don't need to state this explicitly but . . . I am not advocating prohibition. I want to abolish the *desire* for drugs and alcohol, to obliterate the craving for (and dependence on) mind-depleting chemicals.

A caged bear elicits sadness, but a bear that *wants* the prison depresses me. A flightless eagle summons pity; an eagle that chooses the dust is heart-breaking. I want eagles to delight in flight, not birds forced to fly, or punished for slithering.

Similarly, I want a society that considers women to be noble, worthy of respect, equal contributors, not merely a culture that punishes sexist acts. I want us to see all ethnicities as equally human, not a society that pays only legal lip service to the oneness of humankind. I hope our religious factions can, at least, see the beauty in another Faith. I don't want them legislated into doing so. We must rise above merely tolerating each other's existence. I want humanity to venerate health, nobility, sacrificial love and rationality, not be legally prohibited from ingesting what destroys these exalted attributes.

I don't get tipsy, I drink for the taste

I have to address another peculiar reply: 'I don't drink to get drunk. I just like the taste.' To this, I respond: 'Ok. Do you like iced tea? Pineapple juice? Pop? Apple cider? How about lemonade?'

If people don't drink to get drunk or even *tipsy*, then liquor would be on par with iced tea, lemonade, or coffee. Some people do claim they choose alcoholic beverages independent of intoxicating effects. Very well. If true this would mean, 'I'm not interested in the alcohol content.' Okay then, let's do a thought experiment. . .

You like cantaloupe, but discover it increases spousal abuse; would you stop eating it? You love to smell daisies, but learn it harms children when you do. Would you cut out daisy sniffing? I hope so. It's a small inconvenience. You adore pesto sauce on your pasta, but discover everyone's IQ plummets when they ingest it. Would you opt for marinara or alfredo? If you knew someone who, in spite of this knowledge, continued to eat cantaloupe, pesto sauce and smell daisies, would it perplex you?

You crave cantaloupe. You adore daisies. You prefer pesto. But at the same time, you also enjoy honeydew melon, daffodils and alfredo sauce. So, there you go. Tonight's menu: iced tea, fettuccini alfredo, honeydew melon, with a bouquet of daffodils.

Polluting parliament, sacking CERN and desecrating Darwin

If you still feel I miss the mark, that my arrows hit only drunkards, but not the common, responsible drinker, please consider the following.

On a visit to your nation's capital, you find the parliament buildings covered in graffiti, its front steps piled with garbage. How do you feel? Imagine you learn that vandals do this frequently? Would you be angry (perhaps saddened) that people deface the symbol of your democratic system? Many would be furious, even outraged at the desecration. Why? What's the big deal? They are, after all, mere buildings. Vandalism won't impede government, will it? Workers will clean it, probably within a day or two. Then why the fury? Why the sorrow?

I suggest anger, sadness or disgust surfaces because we recognize the absence of veneration in the vandals' violation for the country's political institutions. The physical structures of government embody a concept, an idea and an ideal. The importance lies in their meaning, not the material construction.

Yet, the vandals mar the meaning along with the edifice – the *conceptual* damaged via the concrete. The damage – if allowed to remain – would affect how visitors view it and us. Understandably then, foreigners might question our esteem for our government. If we deface our parliament buildings, we must care little for the processes they represent. I don't think this would be an unfair assumption either. Moreover, our own reverence for government may wane. Prolonged disregard for parliament's seat might lower the public's regard for parliament. If we carried out legislation in a tarnished and derelict building, this might (I suggest would) alter citizens' psychology, resulting in reduced respect. Either we clean up parliament, or people's perception adjusts. We'd modify our opinion instead of the buildings, because they are not *merely* buildings.

If science commands greater value for you, imagine visiting CERN, the European Laboratory for Particle Physics, home to a monumental particle accelerator – the Large Hadron Collider. You walk its corridors to admire devices that explore the limits of reality, that lift the veil of ignorance. Upon entering these hallowed halls of science, you're hit by a putrid stench. Looking around, you see massive piles of cow feces. For some bizarre reason, locals now dump manure in the corridors of CERN. Assume this manure doesn't alter CERN's operation. Physicists walk around the piles, clean their shoes and plug their noses; would you still be sad, outraged, aghast, or disheartened? I would.

But consider why. What if CERN's director told you, 'Not to worry, the janitors will clean it up on Saturday. Besides, we can still do our work'? Would this lessen your exasperation? Would you sanction the director's stance? 'Well, no harm done I guess,' you might say. If not, why not?

I would disapprove, strongly. A soiled CERN disgraces the scientific endeavour, demeans human rationality as a whole. Allowing this centre of research, an emblem of exploration, to be tarnished is unbecoming our power to probe the universe.

Despite a concern for overkill, imagine one final scenario . . .

On Friday, your government gathers 100,000 copies of Charles Darwin's *On the Origin of the Species*, brings them to the capital city, and burns them. Would *this* anger you or cause sorrow? If so, would the fury fizzle out if the government printed more copies, replacing them Monday morning? I think (and hope) this wouldn't diminish your indignation.

Burning Darwin's work, dumping manure in CERN,

vandalizing parliament won't directly impede biology, particle physics, or government. It reveals, however, scant reverence for human intellect, and therefore, the human station; a hiker who finds garbage in an alpine glade justifiably judges the responsible party disrespectful towards Mother Nature. As well, it is not a matter of how much or how long it lasts.

I feel this way about chemical pastimes. Graffiti on parliament shocks me less than vandalism to human minds. Piling manure in CERN can't compare to the dung dumped each weekend in its originating organ: the human brain. Forget CERN's corridors, what about *the creator* of particle physics: reason? Burning Darwin's masterpiece is a tragedy, but we torch countless minds every weekend. But yes – I know – we *reprint* them Monday morning. I find little solace in this fact.

We vandalize, burn and dump garbage in the Temple of the Mind. If you'd censure defiling parliament, scientific institutions, or works of systematic insight, desecrating the Temple of the Mind – *that which birthed them all* – should cut your heart.

The world requires renewed reverence for reason. We need a global campaign for the veneration of critical thought. Our future depends on it. Yet how can we soar in the skies, when society joyfully clips its wings? Just as polluting parliament, staining CERN or desecrating Darwin prevent us from realizing their import, ransacking the Temple of the Mind retards our progress profoundly. It demonstrates that we don't value clear thinking. Worse, it devalues it, daily in this case.

The two wings of the human reality

I must confess. I waited until the Temple of the Mind to speak of sacking CERN, flightless eagles, the human emblem and Purdy the confused peacock. Yes, mind is humankind's peacock tail – a crucial and defining quality. I postponed the point because we easily extol intellect, but hesitate to equally exalt virtue. 'Abdu'l-Bahá speaks powerfully of humanity's moral nature. Deny this defining feature, and we deny our nature. Remove this facet, and we remove our station as human beings. Let's reflect on His words:

> To look after one's self only is, therefore, an animal propensity. It is the animal propensity to live solitary and alone. It is the animal proclivity to look after one's own comfort. But man was created to be a man – to be fair, to be just, to be merciful, to be kind to all his species, never to be willing that he himself be well off while others are in misery and distress. This is an attribute of the animal and not of man. Nay, rather, man should be willing to accept hardships for himself in order that others may enjoy wealth; he should enjoy trouble for himself that others may enjoy happiness and well-being. This is the attribute of man. This is becoming of man. Otherwise man is not man – he is less than the animal.[9]

'Abdu'l-Bahá clearly states that if we remove altruism and self-sacrifice – defining human qualities – we become 'less than the animal'. Remove these qualities, we transmute gold to lead, like some deranged anti-alchemist.

> The man who thinks only of himself and is thoughtless of others is undoubtedly inferior to the animal because the animal is not possessed of the reasoning faculty. The animal is excused; but in man there is reason, the faculty of justice, the faculty of mercifulness. Possessing all these faculties, he must not leave them unused. He who is so hard-hearted as to think only of his own comfort, such an one will not be called man.
> Man is he who forgets his own interests for the sake of others. His own comfort he forfeits for the well-being of all.

Nay, rather, his own life must he be willing to forfeit for the life of mankind. Such a man is the honor of the world of humanity. Such a man is the glory of the world of mankind. Such a man is the one who wins eternal bliss. Such a man is near to the threshold of God. Such a man is the very manifestation of eternal happiness . . .[10]

So, the 'animal is excused' because it lacks 'the reasoning faculty'. Yet God holds mankind responsible because we combine reason with 'the faculty of justice' and mercifulness – the fruits of *Mind* and *Heart*. Joined, these faculties summon the admiration of all. We must look up to what we can be, extol all that is beautiful in humankind. 'Abdu'l-Bahá continues:

Consider how the greatest men in the world – whether among prophets or philosophers – all have forfeited their own comfort, have sacrificed their own pleasure for the well-being of humanity. They have sacrificed their own lives for the body politic. They have sacrificed their own wealth for that of the general welfare. They have forfeited their own honor for the honor of mankind. Therefore, it becomes evident that this is the highest attainment for the world of humanity.[11]

Both Temples – *Heart* and *Mind* – define humanity. Intellect is our crimson-coloured petals; virtue, our floral fragrance. Humanity soars upward on these two wings: love and reason. Our hearts radiate as much as our intellects.

The point and the bottom bar

The Temple of the Mind hums with hymns to rationality and reason. At this Temple, we celebrate cogent thought and clear consideration. If we value reason – our defining feature, our emblem – why eclipse its radiance for even an instant? Why willingly stain what makes us *truly* beautiful, and yet be more worried with personal hygiene, grooming or garments? Why tear down the Temple, even if it can be rebuilt in a day; why scar it for a second? To cite a blemish's transitory nature both misses the point and displays scant respect for reason.

Once again, I offer a *bottom bar*. If you use recreational chemicals – and that is your free choice – please esteem those who don't. Don't view them with confusion, pity or disdain. Admire abstainers; they – even if unwittingly – live congruently with reason's beauty. We must love the human mind, our flowery fragrance, our peacock's tail, our ferocious roar. Encourage those who seek to conserve this cultural relic: The Temple of the Mind.

5

The Temple of the Soul

We leave behind the former Temples of Body, Heart and Mind. On our tour, we now approach the Temple of the Soul. Its elegance astounds anyone willing to contemplate its craftsmanship; its potential to inspire is underestimated. The Temple's Architect dedicated this shrine to our innate spiritual qualities, qualities perhaps too seldom studied and pondered. To express its relevance to our discussion, I offer the following parable.

A question for Rumi, and The Bedouin's Response

I've adapted the following story to express an unexpected – and perhaps initially confusing – perspective. I added what I will call *The Bedouin's Response*. The central character is the Islamic mystic and philosopher-poet, known as Rumi.

A Question for Rumi:

Rumi strolled through the marketplace. Suddenly, a young man stopped him and made a fervent request: 'Dear Rumi, please explain why in Islam we cannot drink wine. I love the gift of the grape, find joy therein and cannot understand the prohibition.'

Rumi responded: 'My friend, if the wine drinker be gentle, if he is kind and compassionate, loving and joyful these will show when the wine takes him. But, if anger and arrogance hide within, these emerge, and since most people harbor the brute within, wine is forbidden to everyone.'

The Bedouin's Response

The young man paused, mulling over the response, agreement and confusion both present on his face. As he pondered, a nearby Bedouin joined the two men. He asked, 'May I offer another perspective?' The young man nodded. Rumi gestured to the desert dweller, inviting the response.

'Dear friend, Rumi speaks truthfully. Wine may draw forth hidden anger or violence, may unmask buried pride or crudeness. No doubt the brute sleeps in all of us. But Islam also forbids wine to protect us from a subtler threat.'

The young man nodded, urging the Bedouin to continue.

'If a man be gentle, happy, and humble, the wine may increase his gentleness, joy and humility. He may, while subject to grape's nectar, become kinder, more social and joyful. It is *also* for *this* reason that God forbids wine.'

The questioner dwelt in thought for a moment. Slowly, a smile filled his face. Then, he turned to the Bedouin, took the old man's hand, said, 'Thank you so much!' and walked away into the crowd.

After agreeing with Rumi, the Bedouin proposed that God also forbids wine because it can increase humility, kindness, sociability and joy. Why fault these charming results? Why quell compassion or tenderness? I raise this because most would give Rumi's answer. To me, the answer is incomplete without the Bedouin's response.

This story conveys truths that troubled me deeply as a young man. The tale encapsulates my battle with drugs and alcohol. I cherished these substances because people would open up, speak livelier, rejoice and (at times) discuss topics they avoided when sober. This final quality dominated my love of liquor.

When I say people displayed courage towards taboo topics, I do not mean they opened up about matters sexual, vulgar or offensive. Nowadays, many don't need intoxicants to do that. Rather, I found they would finally discuss the opposite: meaningful topics – their passions, life's purpose, their dreams, human potential and the person they hoped to one day become.

Many people, tight-lipped in sobriety, emerged from their social cages to air their longing for meaning and self-development. Further, they often burst forth in expressions of love and admiration, pouring forth feelings of affection, now unhindered by social inhibitions. I came to realize the venues where philosophy flowed more freely were often soaked in booze or shrouded by drugs. Early on, this caused me joy; later however, deep sadness. My sorrow arose from an awareness about my own chemical use, and like the Rumi story, it will sound odd.

The lily in the muck

Bahá'u'lláh's work *The Seven Valleys* lays out stages on the journey to reunion with the Beloved: God. It recounts the voyage to our heavenly homeland. In the Valley of Search, Bahá'u'lláh relates a stage, or state of being, the seeker will reach.

In this journey the seeker reacheth a station wherein he seeth all created things wandering distracted in search of the Friend. How many a Jacob will he see searching after his Joseph, how many a lover will he behold hastening towards the Well-Beloved; a world of adoring souls will he witness tracing the path of the Adored One![1]

The Biblical Jacob longed for his lost son Joseph; we long for reunion with the Divine Friend – God. Yet, we wander distracted, choosing paths that never lead to Him. Thus, every soul seeks the Friend – God – *no matter what we are doing*. Every act, no matter how strange (or seemingly degraded), is a beautiful intention twisted into a confused form. Longing for the *water of life*, we attempt to satiate our thirst with dust and filth – sucking sand we believe to be an oasis.

At our tour's beginning, I offered reasons why people use drugs and alcohol – social confidence, release from pain, an easing of tensions. These goals are sensible. Who would object? Who could condemn the desire for comfort, joy and ease? We rightly regard them as natural desires, beautiful ambitions. The desire is not the problem.

Picture a large swamp, its water stagnant, murky and foul. But in the mire's centre rises an exquisite flower – a white lily. It rests in the midpoint, its flawless petals gleaming in the sunlight, an image of elegance in an otherwise rancid region.

The drinker's intentions – confidence, peace, joy, ease – are the lily flower, admirable, beautiful, desired by all. The *means* to acquire them, however, is the decaying, murky swamp. We long to inhale the lily's fragrance, but instead sniff stagnant muck.

Undeniably, the goals are glorious, but we can't catch them with chemicals. When we use alcohol or drugs, we 'wander distracted'. We turn from the lily, and confused, wade off into the swamp. We must follow the lily's scent and form – the true intention. This applies to our own actions, as well as when assessing those of others.

Possibly, suggesting we reorient our desires towards God elicits tired sighs, or even scorn. If so, rather than mystical union with God, we can focus on achieving these goals – social comfort, having fun, ease of stress, etc. The method, however, would be to develop them internally, to cultivate our inner strengths, instead of atrophying them by leaning on a chemical crutch.

The muscles of virtue: Cutting off the chemical cast

Our bodies grow under the pressure of load. Push our limits lifting weights, and our muscles develop. Strain our endurance levels, and we extend our physical frontiers; so too with the human spirit. Virtues – love, justice, honesty, kindness – mirror muscular and cardiovascular development. They develop through struggle, even pain. No other way exists. If someone claimed to be generous, but never put forward effort on this front, would you agree?

No one grows strong by lifting feathers in the gym. Nor does one become deeply responsible, loving, confident or forgiving without strain and sacrifice. To evolve, we must push through our limitations; why would we expect it to be otherwise?

What happens, however, when muscles lie idle, unused, their potential unexpressed? We witness the consequence whenever a person breaks a limb. The doctor supports the injured extremity with a cast, allowing the bone to fuse. This provides the stability the limb needs to heal. Leave the cast on, however, and the limb atrophies, becoming weaker with each passing day. The source of stability becomes the *reason* the muscle mass dwindles. The support shrivels what it's meant to protect and heal. Lack of use withers the body – and the heart, and the mind, and the soul.

I wager that this, upon reflection, will likely not seem odd at all. The Bedouin offered this answer in the Rumi story, and 'Abdu'l-Bahá stated this during His talks in Paris:

For if the spiritual qualities of the soul, open to the breath of the Divine Spirit, are never used, they become atrophied, enfeebled, and at last incapable . . . If, on the contrary, the spiritual nature of the soul has been so strengthened that it holds the material side in subjection, then does the man approach the Divine; his humanity becomes so glorified that the virtues of the Celestial Assembly are manifested in him; he radiates the Mercy of God, he stimulates the spiritual progress of mankind, for he becomes a lamp to show light on their path.[2]

The Bedouin, in principle, answered the young man:

Of course, alcohol draws out destructive behaviours, but we *easily* recognize these as harmful. Chemical crutches, however, are deceptive. They fool you, stealing the very qualities that drive you to use them. Drugs' negative effects resemble the harsh desert, clearly menacing, obviously perilous. The chemical crutch's positive effects are a mirage, drawing you deeper into the desert, making you believe water waits. You think you find joy, ease, and comfort, even connection, but chemical pastimes lead us towards the mirage, away from the oasis we seek.

Years ago, I told friends (on multiple occasions) that I wanted to stop smoking marijuana. I wanted freedom from the chemical cast that I knew weakened my psyche. I believed this crutch – marijuana – atrophied my inner abilities. Holding up a joint, I'd say to myself, 'If I get high from this green leaf, I won't have to get it the natural way – by achievement, insight, learning, or truly expressing myself!'

Alcohol was identical. Sure, I felt more fluid socially after a couple of beers. But I wanted *me* to be *truly* confident, not supported by a chemical. Yes, I loved how people opened up and expressed themselves more on liquid courage. But I longed for them to shatter psychological fetters and remove the source of atrophy. Suddenly, I saw chemical crutches everywhere, crutches shrivelling psyches I loved. We needed to evolve, to develop love, confidence, courage and comfort without the use of props. I realized if I wanted to grow, I had to cut off the chemical cast.

We must unearth the *real* virtues within. They must be mined out, not presented on a platter. Lacking the exercise of will, absent sacrifice, alcohol's gifts are burdens. They are illusory. Alcohol outsources what we long for, perpetuating our inability to truly flourish; it places strength in the crutch or the cast, instead of our character. Alcohol's pseudo-gifts distract us, like a multi-sense mirage. We believe we're drinking water, while our bodies waste away, growing weaker, as we fill our mouths with sand.

The Bedouin said that alcohol does not uncover beauty in us, even when it seems to. It tricks us into thinking we've reached our destination. Thinking we've found the lily, we slog around in sludge; led astray by wraiths, we slog deeper into a stagnant swamp.

Lost opportunities

The Bedouin grieved lost opportunities, occasions for evolution. Each time we use chemical supports instead of surmounting obstacles, we lose the prospect of growth. We could evolve intellectually, physically, emotionally or morally, but the chemical crutch misleads us, even weakens us. So, openings for development close when we choose the crutch instead of a crucible. The analogy of crucible – a situation that forces people to grow – proves apt.

Without the liquid-courage crutch, we'd be forced to navigate social gatherings sober. We would, therefore, have to grow psychologically, emotionally and socially. The crutch that keeps us upright paradoxically lays us low. Without chemicals to cushion stress, we'd manage our emotions, and grow mightier with each conquest. But if we hobble past the evolutionary rough road, choosing instead a path of ease, we squander chances to cultivate superior self-discipline. Chemical pastimes offer fun on tap (or inhalation or injection). Yet they make us swerve from pathways of progress.

Our potential summons us to peace, to joy, to love, to a sense of relief. We must nurture these naturally, however, to make them authentically ours. Undeniably, sacrifice, trials and pain await if we seek social ease, peace of mind, and joy without psychological pick-me-ups. Yet it is the pain of discipline and, therefore, of growth. Chemical crutches ignore this reality of life.

6

Ulysses and the Island of the Lotus-Eaters

In Homer's Greek epic, *The Odyssey*, Ulysses and his crew reach the Island of the Lotus-Eaters. Its inhabitants ingest a plant that dispels sorrow and unease. Ulysses' crew then become trapped, ensnared by grief's absence, and freedom from concern. Homer tells us of the crew's island sojourn:

> They started at once, and went about among the Lotus-eaters, who did them no hurt, but gave them to eat of the lotus, which was so delicious that those who ate of it left off caring about home, and did not even want to go back and say what had happened to them, but were for staying and munching lotus with the Lotus-eaters without thinking further of their return.[1]

Oddly, Ulysses claims the Lotus-eaters 'did them no hurt'. but then continues:

> nevertheless, though they wept bitterly I forced them back to the ships and made them fast under the benches. Then I told the rest to go on board at once, lest any of them should taste of the lotus and leave off wanting to get home, so they took their places and smote the grey sea with their oars.[2]

So, Ulysses asserts the Lotus-eaters did his crew no harm, yet he 'forced them back to the ships', tied them under benches, and fled from the island. Why drive the men back, lash them to the ship and flee an island if no harm exists? The confusion derives from the Lotus's illusory gift – joy and ease – for its *gift* was poison, not prize.

Sadly, we live in lotus-eater land. Our society eulogizes chemical sweetness – the relief and joy, the loss of cares, the social fluidity, the work-week's weight eased off. Surely, I will not force friends to the ship and lash them to the benches. Yet danger lurks in the drugs' delights, a delight that robs us of *true* freedom.

Reframing freedom

People generally perceive abstinence as a loss of freedom. Viewed as restriction, it triggers psychological claustrophobia. We feel confined. Hence, caged by perceived prohibition, we lash out. We sense tyranny in the prohibition, the tyranny of a foreign power: abstinence is incarceration, it seems. Understandably so, because we define *freedom* as the absence of constraints. So, I truly empathize with the ensuing anxiety when we hear the declaration: Thou shalt not . . .

Who wouldn't?

Yet, folly lurks in this phobia of restrictions, for it wars with other beliefs we know to be true. If we listen carefully, the voice of prohibition conceals the command of conscience. The ethical call-to-arms – good thoughts, good words, good deeds – demands constraints. In fact, we accomplish ethical progress – be it individual or collective – through limiting what we think, say and, most especially, by what we do.

Hearing this, we sense the footsteps of Orwellian thought-police, moral censors leap into our semi-neurotic minds. But progress necessitates sacrifice, especially moral progress.

Morality demands restrictions, a loss of certain freedoms; there's no avoiding this conclusion. Anyone who's been around children should be well aware of this balance. We do not escape it with age; if anything, we should be able to bear a heavier load than we demand of our children.

To solve any ethical problem – human trafficking, child poverty, starvation, environmental degradation, or global chemical dependence – we must accept behavioural boundaries. When we condemned environmental pollution, we accepted restrictions. We no longer throw fast-food containers out the car window, toss garbage into the streets, or dump sewage in our streams. We accepted laws governing chemical use, began testing and limiting industrial emissions, and outlawed many products. When we acknowledged that people deserve equitable compensation for labour or ingenuity, we no longer disregarded contracts and property entitlements, and granted workers' rights. To protect these rights, we enshrined restraints and controls on behaviour. By acknowledging the immorality of racial, religious and gender discrimination, we accepted limits on what we can say and do. Hopefully, we will one day cleanse our thoughts as well; an ounce of prevention, as it were.

Examine any ethical evolution and you will discover a web of *restrictions* supporting the freedoms we now cherish. In addition, you will find generations who ceased thinking, speaking and acting in diverse ways. Moral progress is the child of restriction; our liberty, the offspring of abstinence.

To evolve as a species, we must evolve our understanding of *freedom* and *restriction*. We must relinquish our phobia of 'Thou shalt not . . .' and hear therein the simultaneous 'You will be able to . . .' Freedom is not *lack of* limitations; it is the *presence* of the right restrictions. The document *One Common Faith* released by the Bahá'í World Centre makes this clear:

By its very nature, unity requires self-sacrifice. '. . . self-love', the Master states, 'is kneaded into the very clay of man'. The ego, termed by Him the 'insistent self', resists instinctively constraints imposed on what it conceives to be its freedom.[3]

Our lower nature (the 'insistent self') resists 'instinctively' what it 'conceives' to be restrictions on its freedom. Our lower nature – the brute within – fears bondage when it sees ropes, but some ropes moor us on the coasts of a better world.

Freedom found in confinement

> Seek freedom and become captive of your desires.
> Seek discipline and find your liberty.
>
> *Frank Herbert*[4]

We understand *restriction* to mean 'whatever limits my desires'. While apparently reasonable, this definition overlooks how we evolve through sacrifice, restricting our time, narrowing our choices, by limiting our desires. Yet these limitations open up new experiences and greater self-expression. Freedom doesn't come from lack of constraint; liberty demands restrictions. Only if we forgo *certain* freedoms can true liberty emerge.

My friend Aleks plays guitar exquisitely, conveying whatever melody meanders through his mind, his heart expressed through sound. To behold it is breathtaking. The freedom he exhibits summons my admiration, and – to be honest – my envy.

Obviously, Aleks was not born a skilled musician; he struggled to scale the heights of musical mastery. He sacrificed hours and hours, days, weeks, months and years to acquire his craft. While his friends played video games, he practised until his fingers hurt. Coworkers relaxed; Aleks drilled musical scales.

Family members took it easy; Aleks played – the same riff – over and over. Of course, he got tired, even disheartened, on his journey. Yet these sacrifices, these restrictions, carved out his current capacity. He accepted limitations for a higher goal, limitations that now grant great freedom.

My dear friend Jamen is a martial arts master. I studied with him for over a decade. During that time, he continually awed me with his ability to dominate my centre of gravity, move me effortlessly, counter my attacks, and strike at will with blistering precision. His physical mastery astounds all who experience it. No one would deny that his skills give him great freedom. The freedom he displays, however, is the offspring of abstinences.

Jamen gave up endless hours. He slaved for decades to become a senior full instructor in numerous martial arts. He forfeited sleep and leisure, and bled for his mastery – literally. I trained with Jamen seven days a week, hours each day, and when I left exhausted, Jamen trained on. His friends relaxed on couches; Jamen wrestled on mats. Buddies went for a swim; Jamen sweated in a gym. Pals sat around; Jamen sacrificed – for decades.

Pablo de Sarasate was a famous 19th-century violinist and composer. People often attribute the following quotation to him: 'A genius! For 37 years, I've practised fourteen hours a day, and now they call me a genius!'[5] Whether he said it or not, we all know mastery demands sacrifice, and bestows delectable fruit. Think of a person fluent in a second or third language. A new world of literature, music, poetry, history and philosophy opens up to them. They have access to millions more hearts and minds, access denied those who are linguistically limited. Watch an accomplished gymnast. They flip, pivot and leap, their bodies achieving a precision I can scarcely imagine. Consider those deeply versed in mathematics, chemistry, history, political science, physics or photography. Adept in their chosen fields, they create, understand, dialogue on, portray or capture the world in precise and picturesque ways. And they all hold in common one feature: the loss of certain freedoms in exchange for others. An exchange they all knowingly and willing performed.

Yet through loss, they gain; by restriction, they become free. Relinquishing lesser freedoms, we acquire higher liberties. Without restrictions, we achieve nothing noble, nothing precious. Further, the lost freedoms appear feeble and colourless compared to the powerful and vibrant liberties gained via sacrifice. In the end, we close freedom's door and open another onto the landscape of liberty. We trade fleeting and grosser pleasures for lasting and subtler joys. We must leave the earth if we wish to soar above it.

In the Hindu Upanishads, Yama, the god of Death, says:

> There is the path of joy and there is the path of pleasure. Both attract the soul. Who follows the first comes to good; who follows pleasure, reaches not the End. The two paths lie in front of man. Pondering on them, the wise man chooses the path of joy; the fool takes the path of pleasure.[6]

The path of pleasure represents lower freedoms; the path of joy, the higher liberties. So, is abstinence from alcohol and drugs a loss of freedom? Of course it is – a 'freedom' I gladly surrender to gain superior, more delectable liberties. I give up video games to learn guitar. I abstain from television to learn philosophy. I give up rest to learn martial arts. My selections aside, I don't think the principle sounds odd, though it can be arduous. I lay leisure on the altar of sacrifice to study languages, learn our world's religious heritage, serve community, and explore the arts and sciences. I lay ephemeral freedoms on that altar so that I may take up lasting liberties.

In the Most Holy Book, Bahá'u'lláh speaks of freedom's paradox:

True liberty consisteth in man's submission unto My commandments, little as ye know it. Were men to observe that which We have sent down unto them from the Heaven of Revelation, they would, of a certainty, attain unto perfect liberty. Happy is the man that hath apprehended the Purpose of God in whatever He hath revealed from the Heaven of His Will that pervadeth all created things. Say: The liberty that profiteth you is to be found nowhere except in complete servitude unto God, the Eternal Truth. Whoso hath tasted of its sweetness will refuse to barter it for all the dominion of earth and heaven.[7]

The point and the bottom bar

The *point*: alcohol's gifts – social fears calmed, stress released, lightness and joy – are splendid, but superficial and fleeting. Mirage-like, chemical pick-me-ups create the illusion that *we* possess these gifts. In doing so, they draw us deeper into a parched desert, further from the waters we seek – the fleeting illusion steals opportunities for growth.

Chemical crutches atrophy our psyches, our hearts and our souls. To achieve anything of worth we must struggle and strive. We must bleed for it. We must train our souls – no performance-enhancing drugs allowed. We must, therefore, accept restrictions to experience true liberty, put ourselves in bondage to be free.

The *bottom bar*: If you opt for chemical crutches, try to see beauty in the abstainer's choice. They walk a path of self-discipline and sacrifice, a path to independence, the route to liberty. You could view them instead as mental, emotional and spiritual athletes who refuse to lean on performance-enhancing drugs, not because they eschew cheating, but because they value natural, sustainable development. Even more, realizing that chemical casts weaken us, respect those dedicated to sobriety. Sobriety expresses an awareness of a cosmic law: true growth demands sacrifice.

7

But What About the Weed?

Grouping marijuana with alcohol and harsher drugs seems unjust. Marijuana seeds no social chaos, spawns no aggression; it soothes the soul, makes us calm and peaceable. Doesn't it? Many people concede (albeit reluctantly) that alcohol – or its more putrid pals: cocaine, ecstasy, meth, LSD, etc. – burdens bodies, harms hearts and mars minds. The *happy* weed, however, sings a different song. Marijuana, many believe, is not merely the least problematic drug; it's entirely beneficial.

'What's wrong with it?' versus 'What's good about it?'

I admit that given the choice between booze or weed, I'd take the green leaf without hesitation. But this – in no way – equates to marijuana being *good*. When evaluating anything, too often we ask 'What's wrong with it?' instead of, 'What's good about it?' Yet much hangs on the difference. We shouldn't limit ourselves to determining detriments, attending only to undesirable consequences. Rather, we should ask what benefits, blessings or bounties it bestows on us and society. Many acts may not be intrinsically immoral. But at the same time, they offer no beauty, perform no positive function; they are inert.

If we seek either – detriments or benefits – we must

investigate and (at least) abide by the principle of minimal research. As before, I don't stake my argument on the information's absolute accuracy; I only wish to show that potentially damning data lies easily in reach. With a brief survey in hand, we'll take a whirlwind tour of the Temples. Then, when people ask 'What's wrong with it?' we can, first of all, ask, 'Have you looked?' When considering alcohol, I performed a modest Internet search to see what rises to the surface; I adopted the same method with marijuana. Would the average person be able to uncover reasons to abstain? Yes. We find readily accessible and negative information, information often ignored. In this case, however, let's first explore the benefits of marijuana.

The Temple of the Body

Does marijuana have medicinal properties? Can it help people? Marijuana's street advocates occasionally present it as a panacea – a remedy for all ills. No doubt, this is absurd, and indicative of addiction. Yet denying the panacea-property shouldn't blind us to its actual benefits. The UK's Royal College of General Practitioners states the following:

> There is evidence that it is effective against chemotherapy induced nausea and vomiting and as an analgesic and that it is valuable for combating the loss of appetite and weight loss experienced in patients with cancer and AIDS, for the relief of muscle spasms in patients with multiple sclerosis and in the treatment of glaucoma. Randomised controlled trials designed to compare cannabis with existing treatment will show if cannabis proves superior to existing remedies and, if so, there should be no bar to it being made available to appropriate patients in the appropriate formulation.[1]

An author for Harvard University's Medical School confirms marijuana's potential benefits:

> While marijuana isn't strong enough for severe pain (for example, post-surgical pain or a broken bone), it is quite effective for the chronic pain that plagues millions of Americans, especially as they age . . .
>
> In particular, marijuana appears to ease the pain of multiple sclerosis, and nerve pain in general . . .
>
> Along these lines, marijuana is said to be a fantastic muscle relaxant, and people swear by its ability to lessen tremors in Parkinson's disease. I have also heard of its use quite successfully for fibromyalgia, endometriosis, interstitial cystitis, and most other conditions where the final common pathway is chronic pain.
>
> Marijuana is also used to manage nausea and weight loss, and can be used to treat glaucoma. A highly promising area of research is its use for PTSD in veterans who are returning from combat zones. Many veterans and their therapists report drastic improvement and clamor for more studies, and for a loosening of governmental restrictions on its study. Medical marijuana is also reported to help patients suffering from pain and wasting syndrome associated with HIV, as well as irritable bowel syndrome and Crohn's disease.[2]

We find similar statements from the World Health Organization (WHO):

> Several studies have demonstrated the therapeutic effects of cannabinoids for nausea and vomiting in the advanced stages of illnesses such as cancer and AIDS. Dronabinol (tetrahydrocannabinol) has been available by prescription for more than a decade in the USA. Other therapeutic uses of cannabinoids

are being demonstrated by controlled studies, including treatment of asthma and glaucoma, as an antidepressant, appetite stimulant, anticonvulsant and antispasmodic, research in this area should continue.[3]

Consider statements made by the Centers for Disease Control and Prevention (CDC):

Studies of man-made forms of the chemicals found in the marijuana plant can be helpful in treating nausea and vomiting from cancer chemotherapy. Studies have found that marijuana can be helpful in treating neuropathic pain (pain caused by damaged nerves).[4]

These sources offer a majestic roster of marijuana's benefits. They reference its therapeutic use in treating issues related to:

- Cancer
- Aids
- Multiple sclerosis
- Glaucoma
- Chronic pain
- Nerve pain
- Depression
- Asthma

As well, they express potential benefits for:

- Fibromyalgia
- Endometriosis
- Interstitial cystitis
- Post-traumatic stress (PTSD)

These groups understandably call for relaxed governmental controls to increase study of marijuana's therapeutic applications.

Bahá'í texts and medicinal marijuana

Unsurprisingly – I hope – Bahá'í scriptures unequivocally approve of medicinal drugs:

> It should be noted that the above prohibition against taking certain classes of drugs does not forbid their use when prescribed by qualified physicians as part of a medical treatment.[5]

Put simply: no Bahá'í would (or should) object to chemicals for medical use. Yet the context of this quotation proves illuminating. The 'classes of drugs' referred to are, in fact, opium and hashish – opioids and marijuana!

Bahá'ís support, therefore, the medicinal application of opium and cannabis. Yet when used as chemical pastimes, the Bahá'í Writings are exceedingly direct. Speaking of opium, 'Abdu'l-Bahá states that it is 'foul and accursed', that it 'layeth in ruins the very foundation of what it is to be human', and is a 'most powerful of plagues'.[6] The same reference from the Most Holy Book also cites 'hallucinogenic agents such as LSD, peyote and similar substances' which fall – it *seems* clear – under the principle of medicinal applications when prescribed by qualified physicians. To be clear: the medical sources above – WHO, CDC, etc. – echo a principle put forth by the Bahá'í Central Figures over a century and a half ago.

I suspect all drugs – including peyote, opiates, psilocybin (magic mushrooms), ayahuasca (DMT), etc. – possess potentially positive properties, capable of serving humankind in therapeutic ways. However, 'qualified physicians' ought to prescribe and monitor them 'as part of a medical treatment'. So, for now, let's assume marijuana has zero negative effects, only positive properties. Does this recommend recreational use? No. This is the Bahá'í Faith's central principle regarding any substance's therapeutic use.

Many pharmaceuticals alleviate undesired symptoms, but we don't encourage using them for fun. Morphine may be a blessing to those in pain, but this gives no green light to the heroin or opioid user. Prozac or Paxil alleviate depression, but I wouldn't propose popping them for pleasure. We use Valium and Atavan to treat anxiety; as a social practice, they're a bad idea. Haldol and Risperdal control psychotic disorders and low doses are used with Tourette's Syndrome. As someone with Tourette's Syndrome, I'm familiar with these drugs and wouldn't suggest attending Haldol or Risperdal parties. I have used Zopiclone to manage insomnia; works like a charm, but don't pop it for amusement. Pharmaceuticals relieve health and mental disorders. We do not, however, automatically assume they're suitable for fun.

So, marijuana may alleviate ailments – its medicinal use. Yet we also employ chemotherapy, invasive surgery, and semi-debilitating drugs (think of schizophrenia, Tourette's Syndrome, bi-polar disorder, etc.). These interventions aren't *good* for the person; they are *less bad*. No one advocates the recreational use of chemotherapy, anti-psychotics, self-surgery or lithium. Listing a drug's medicinal benefits in no way recommends its recreational use; this is a non-sequitur – the conclusion does not follow from the argument. A similar logical error occurs when discussing hemp.

Separating 'hemp' from 'high'

Hemp – marijuana's cousin – offers many benefits. We can use it for textiles, biomass fuels, paper products, biodegradable plastics, etc. This would alleviate environmental pressure and benefit industry. As a layman, I believe the benefits of hemp worthy of serious consideration.

Curiously, such benefits often arise during disputes about marijuana. I find this odd because it's wholly irrelevant to the debate. Hemp has little or no psychoactive effects; you don't get high on hemp. A plant used for environmentally-friendly industry has no connection with smoking a related species to get high.

Yet even if only marijuana existed, and it provided all hemp's material benefits, the argument still fails. If marijuana produced thousands more products than hemp, would this justify getting stoned? . . . Of course not.

Diesel fuel propels cars. But this offers no justification for huffing it to get high. It's great for mileage – not so beneficial to bodies and brains. Many chemicals aid in the creation of paints; but I wouldn't sniff them at a party – even if they *were* environmentally-friendly paints. We can use cocaine as an anaesthetic for nose surgeries – but shouldn't snort it for fun. Glass products are clearly useful; yet if we discovered you could get a buzz by sniffing powdered glass, this wouldn't justify the practice of '*glassing*'. Simply put, hemp's benefits can't justify marijuana's recreational use; it's a complete non-sequitur.

An identical confusion surrounds cannabinoid (CBD) use. Many cited benefits of marijuana, in fact, come from a chemical found in both marijuana and hemp: cannabinoids. As the Mayo Clinic states: 'CBD doesn't contain tetrahydrocannabinol (THC), the psychoactive ingredient found in marijuana that produces a high.'[7]

This is why policy-makers separate cannabis from CBDs:

So far, researchers haven't conducted enough large-scale clinical trials that show that the benefits of the marijuana plant (as opposed to its cannabinoid ingredients) outweigh its risks in patients it's meant to treat.[8]

Given that CBD can be separated from THC, therefore, I could have named this section: Separating 'CBDs' from 'Stoned'.

But there is 'the bad'

The above sources cite health benefits. Do they also report negative aspects? Yes. The WHO reports:

> It was found that cannabis impaired all capabilities of learning, including associative processes, and psychomotor performance. The only areas that were not affected were those of abstraction and vocabulary . . .
>
> Consistent with earlier observations, numerous studies in the past ten years have confirmed that cannabis impairs psychomotor performance in a wide variety of tasks, such as handwriting, tests of motor coordination, divided-attention, digit-symbol substitution, and operant tasks of various types . . .[9]

> The relatively small number of experimental studies carried out since the previous WHO report have confirmed that cannabis can impair various components of driving behaviour, such as braking time, starting time, and reaction to red lights or other danger signals.[10]

How about the CDC?

> Smoked marijuana delivers THC and other cannabinoids to the body, but it also delivers harmful substances to users and those close by, including many of the same substances found in tobacco smoke, which are harmful to the lungs and

cardiovascular system. So it's hard to separate the effects of the compounds in marijuana on the cardiovascular system from the hazards posed by the irritants and other chemicals contained in the smoke. More research is needed to understand the full impact of marijuana use on the circulatory system to determine if marijuana use leads to higher risk of death from these causes.[11]

Smoked marijuana, in any form, can harm lung tissues and cause scarring and damage to small blood vessels. Smoke from marijuana contains many of the same toxins, irritants, and carcinogens as tobacco smoke. Smoking marijuana can also lead to a greater risk of bronchitis, cough, and phlegm production . . .

Children exposed to the psychoactive compounds in marijuana are potentially at risk for negative health effects, including developmental problems for babies whose mothers used marijuana while pregnant. Other research shows that marijuana use during adolescence can impact the developing teenage brain and cause problems with attention, motivation, and memory.[12]

And they add:

At this time, there is not enough evidence to recommend that patients inhale or ingest marijuana as a treatment for cancer-related symptoms or side effects of cancer therapy.[13]

What about the Royal College of General Practitioners? Two quotations are particularly telling:

A literature search for the health risks of cannabis will reveal numerous academic papers and scores of reviews on the subject yet few general practitioners and fewer still of the public can cite one problem with the commonest illicit substance used today. That cannabis contains at least as many carcinogens as tobacco smoke, that it is used in a way that maximises its harmful effects and that it more than likely contributes to the production of psychosis in young adults may surprise many readers, who like most of the population think that the drug is at worst harmless and at best good for you. It is a credit to the pro-cannabis debate that the legalisation issue has proved such an effective 'smoke screen' to health risks associated with the drug . . .

The known effects of cannabis are analogous to the known effects of alcohol and tobacco, though its dangers are less obvious. The evidence that it produces dependence is beyond dispute, with around 5-10% eventually becoming dependent. Cannabis also impairs concentration, short-term memory, attention and rational thought, impairs driving and piloting skills and amplifies the driving impairments caused by concomitant alcohol use. Larger amounts of cannabis can produce anxiety and depression, psychotic states lasting several days and an increased risk of developing schizophrenia. [14]

The Royal College, therefore, concludes:

The reputation that cannabis is a safe drug is unjustified. The reasons for this misplaced view are that it is not immediately lethal in the way that heroin is, that its effects on mood state are not as obvious as alcohol and that its capacity to produce dependence, like alcohol is slow and insidious and its widespread use is a relatively new phenomena. Recent inquiries on cannabis have come to the same conclusion, that cannabis can be harmful and that its use should be discouraged. [15]

The Royal College of General Practitioners believes cannabis's rosy reputation is 'unjustified', and mentions that 'numerous academic studies and scores of reviews on the subject' testify to this. They lament, however, that 'few general practitioners and fewer still of the public can cite one problem' with marijuana; put simply, the facts are in, but no one's listening.

Marijuana does, obviously, harm the body. We should expect this, given that it's a burnt, dried plant that's inhaled. Even ingested, however, it dulls motor skills and reduces cognition. This too shouldn't surprise anyone.

Consider: you have to reach the airport quickly through dense city traffic. Two friends offer you a ride. One is stoned, the other sober. Concerned with your safety, which would you choose? Would you allow employees to operate machinery high? Would you choose a stoned or straight helicopter pilot?

Further, given a choice between a sober surgeon and one doped up, which would you prefer to operate on your body? Would you allow your stoned martial arts partner to spar with you? When I was a martial arts teacher, I refused to teach students who were high. We could swiftly create a litany of circumstances where anyone would opt for the sober individual. Why? Because marijuana weakens and confuses both body and mind.

Consider a mechanism – car, computer, truck, tractor or dishwasher; imagine it working as intended, smoothly, with clear communication between user and machine. Suddenly, the device slows, its processes somewhat erratic, its lights dimmed, communication (previously clear and direct) now slightly garbled and confused. Would you think it an intriguing new and desirable feature? Or, rather, would you consider it a malfunction: an electrical short-circuit, a part broken or worn, possible water damage or that it just past its warranty date?

The natural interpretation would be that something is wrong. Yet, if you'd lived your entire life around machines that clunked, shook, sent out garbled messages, and performed erratically on a regular basis, you'd think, 'That's just how it is – normal behaviour.' Likewise, with chemical pastimes.

I find the challenge surrounding discussing drug hobbies is pointing out the obvious without causing offence – a battle not for the faint of heart. Yet, the swiftest (and I'd add, surest) means of assessing chemical pastimes is to watch someone use them – free of the veil of normalcy that is. It is analogous to watching a car filled with bleach, a toaster with plasticine, a computer riddled with viruses – a slackening, corroding, disrupting or distorting of its natural function. The beloved happy weed slackens mental speed, distorts rational thought processes, disrupts communication between brain and body and (as we'll soon see) causes dependence and harmful psychological states, especially among adolescents – its most frequent users.

The denial of dependence

Another widespread issue I call '*dependence denial*' – denying marijuana's addictive properties. Of course, this occurs with any drug addiction. Yet usually, addicts acknowledge the drug's addictive powers, but claim *they* could quit at any time. They rarely deny the chemical produces dependence. Marijuana advocates, in contrast, proclaim they're free of the chemical cage *because* pot (we are led to believe) possesses no addictive properties – a claim we can test.

In March of 2016, we find on *Yale News* – as in Yale University:

> A genome-wide analysis of more than 14,000 individuals has identified several gene variants that increase risk of cannabis dependence, a new Yale led study has found. The analysis also suggests that the genetic risk for dependence on marijuana is associated with a higher inherited risk of major depression,

according to the study published March 30 in the journal *JAMA Psychiatry*.

The study was first to identify variants that significantly increase risk for cannabis dependence. It was based on knowledge that, like alcoholism and other addictions, the risk of cannabis dependence can be inherited. The researchers wondered whether those with some forms of mental illness might also be at higher risk of cannabis dependence, as they are for addiction to other abused substances such as alcohol.

'We were surprised to find a genetic risk overlap between cannabis dependence and major depression,' said Dr. Joel Gelernter, the Foundations Fund Professor of Psychiatry, professor of genetics and of neuroscience, and senior author of the study.[16]

Yale University reports on the genetic links between cannabis dependence and mental illness. You can find the original data in *JAMA: Journal of the American Medical Association*. Reading this, I assume they didn't wonder *if* cannabis dependence is real. This makes sense, because they analysed 14,000 people's genomes to study 'gene variants that increase risk of cannabis dependence'.

Consider: the American Medical Association doesn't publish studies of 14,000 genomes for 'gene variants that increase telepathic powers'. Naturally, because they don't believe 'telepathic powers' exist. We have the opposite case with cannabis dependence.

I remember well spending entire days seeking a bag of weed. Many times, I commented on this to friends. We'd devote hours and hours to finding it, smoking it, and then languishing during the comedown: the deterioration of mood and motivation after a high.

The British Journal of Psychiatry contains a paper entitled 'Psychiatric effects of cannabis'. In it, we read:

It had been believed that cannabis use did not lead to tolerance and that there was no withdrawal syndrome. However,
since the mid-1970s, these views have been challenged by
many experimental and observational studies . . .

The cannabis-withdrawal syndrome has now been unequivocally demonstrated and includes restlessness, anxiety,
dysphoria, irritability, insomnia, anorexia, muscle tremor,
increased reflexes and autonomic effects including changes in
heart rate, blood pressure, sweating and diarrhea . . .

Thomas (1996) found that 35% of cannabis users said that
they could not stop when they wanted to, 24% continued
to use despite problems attributed to the drug and 13% felt
that they could not control their consumption. Restlessness
or irritability if they could not use cannabis was reported by
20% of those surveyed . . . With regard to untoward social
consequences, 14% of cannabis users agreed that the consumption of the drug had caused them to neglect activities
previously considered important or enjoyable. [17]

We're told dependence has been 'unequivocally demonstrated'.
Once again, we hear about wasted opportunities, how many
'neglect activities previously considered important or enjoyable'
– a fact I recall too well. In my final years of cannabis use, I
regularly commented on wasted opportunities for growth and
development.

In Ashton's article 'Pharmacology and effects of cannabis: A
brief review', we find the same pattern:

Tolerance has been shown to develop to many effects of cannabis including the high and many systemic effects, and a
cannabis withdrawal syndrome has been clearly demonstrated in controlled studies in both animals and man. The
withdrawal syndrome has similarities to alcohol, opiate and

benzodiazepine withdrawal states and includes restlessness, insomnia, anxiety, increased aggression, anorexia, muscle tremor and autonomic effects.[18]

The National Centre on Addiction and Substance Abuse, at Columbia University, in its paper *Non-Medical Marijuana: Rite of Passage or Russian Roulette?* claimed that:

Nine percent of those who ever use marijuana become dependent on it. In 1996 (the latest year for which numbers are available), more than 195,000 individuals entered treatment for marijuana; 62 percent (more than 120,000) of whom are under age 25, 45 percent (nearly 88,000) are teens or younger. There are more teens and children in treatment for marijuana than for any other substance including alcohol.[19]

A personal note

Regrettably, I didn't need this research. To me, these concepts are experiential, not theoretical. I battled with addiction to marijuana and continually tried to stop – for years. In fact, I quit so many times, it became a joke among friends. Regularly, I'd give my weed to friends, state I didn't want it, and ask them to take it. I repeatedly renounced the foolish green leaf. Eye rolling and sighs often attended my friends' standard reply: 'Are you *sure*, Rob? Ok, we'll keep it for now. But when you want it back, just call us.'

For four straight years, I made that call, sometimes within hours. This became so common one friend would hide it in my house. So, when I called, he could tell me where to find it – immediately.

In the last year of my battle, my roommate Jenny (now my

wife) would listen to me denounce marijuana, condemn its addictive properties, lament how it atrophied my inner world, and distracted from loftier life pursuits. Then, upon hearing our mutual roommate come home, I'd jump up to see if he had a joint.

Each time, she begged me to stop, to be congruent, to heed my own words, and not *smoke up* with him – for a year I failed. To deny dependence is to deny years of experience, and the experience of many friends. If you smoke pot regularly, test this. Stop, and watch your mind.

Weed and the Temple of the Mind

Marijuana's effect on mental performance immediately advocates abstinence. Contrasted with the Temple of the Mind, the *wonderful* weed is a noxious one. Honestly, if you doubt marijuana's negative mental effects, either you've never spoken to someone who's high or the veil of normalcy obscures your vision.

Bahá'u'lláh's prohibition against substances that diminish intelligence – a human emblem – equally applies here. Weed unmistakably mars the mind. It reduces reasoning powers, impairs our intellect, and is ruinous to rational thought. To deny this requires either unfamiliarity or dishonesty.

Imagine: You have a test coming up. You can take it stoned or sober. Which do you choose? How about an important job interview? Would you opt for sobriety or the green leaf? This week, you must participate in a debate – to be high, or not to be high? Sorry, there is no question. Imagine a lawyer defending your child, a judge in charge of a murder trial, or a politician arguing for a vital law that will affect millions – and they're stoned. Would this concern you? Obviously, and for *good reason* – pun intended.

In any situation where your fate depends on swift and cogent thought, which would you choose? The answer is obvious. Nothing more needs to be said; nevertheless, here comes the data.

A publication from the *Journal of Addiction Medicine* states:

> THC intoxication has been shown to impair cognitive function on a number of levels – from basic motor coordination to more complex tasks, such as the ability to plan, organize, solve problems, make decisions, remember, and control emotions and behavior. The higher level cognitive functions, termed executive functions, are critically important, particularly when dealing with novel situations in which decisions must be made . . .[20]

The theme is echoed in the *Indian Journal of Psychiatry*:

> There is a widely held belief that cannabis is inert to the brain, and although the psychological consequences are quite evident, the population at large seems unconvinced. There is much debate about the nature of cannabis dependence, as it is considered non-addicting due to the absence of a withdrawal state. This presumption has also been proved wrong.
>
> The general impression supported by many studies is that cannabis causes cognitive decline, particularly with long-term usage. Majority of studies have suggested a significant cognitive decline in cannabis abusers compared to non-abusers and healthy controls. A report by Bartholomew *et al.* suggested that cannabis use has a detrimental effect on prospective memory ability in young adults but users may not be aware of these deficits. Cannabis is known to produce substantial acute effects on human cognition and visuomotor skills.[21]

A quotation from the Royal College of Psychiatrists paper quoted previously is also worth considering:

> Not surprisingly, cannabis impairs cognitive and psychomotor performance. The effects are similar to those of alcohol and benzodiazepines and include slowing of reaction time, motor incoordination, specific defects in short-term memory, difficulty in concentration and particular impairment in complex tasks which require divided attention. The effects are dose-related but can be demonstrated after relatively small doses (5-10 mg THC in a joint), even in experienced cannabis users, and have been shown in many studies across a wide range of neurocognitive and psychomotor tests. These effects are additive with those of other central nervous system depressants.[22]

Long-term effects of chronic use

> There is considerable evidence, reviewed by Hall *et al* (1994), that performance in heavy, chronic cannabis users remains impaired even when they are not actually intoxicated. These impairments, especially of attention, memory and ability to process complex information, can last for many weeks, months or even years after cessation of cannabis use. Whether or not there is permanent cognitive impairment in heavy long-term users is not clear.[23]

Above, we find a telling phrase: 'Not surprisingly, cannabis impairs cognitive and psychomotor performance.' Honestly, this *cannot* surprise anyone familiar with cannabis. They *may* be startled by the lasting effects 'when they are not actually intoxicated' (my own experience made me nod in agreement). To deny the immediate effects, however, is senseless.

The website *Psychology Today* relates the following information:

> If someone is high on marijuana, he or she might:
> - Seem dizzy and have trouble walking
> - Seem silly and giggly for no reason
> - Have very red, bloodshot eyes
> - Have a hard time remembering things that just happened
> - Become very sleepy after a few hours, as the early effects fade . . .[24]

Marijuana hinders the user's short-term memory (memory for recent events), and he or she may have trouble handling complex tasks. With the use of more potent varieties of marijuana, even simple tasks can be difficult. Because of the drug's effects on perceptions and reaction time, users could be involved in auto crashes . . .[25]

Under the influence of marijuana, students may find it hard to study and learn. Young athletes could find their performances are off; timing, movements and coordination are all affected by THC.[26]

In 2014, the American Psychological Association warned:

> Frequent marijuana use can have a significant negative effect on the brains of teenagers and young adults, including cognitive decline, poor attention and memory, and decreased IQ . . .[27]

They also quote:

'It needs to be emphasized that regular cannabis use, which we consider once a week, is not safe and may result in addiction and neurocognitive damage, especially in youth,' said Krista Lisdahl, PhD, director of the brain imaging and neuropsychology lab at University of Wisconsin-Milwaukee.[28]

Another report from the American Psychological Association expresses concern for the cognitive detriments caused by cannabis use:

Specifically, individuals who never regularly used cannabis had a slight increase (0.8 IQ point) in IQ from childhood into adulthood, while those diagnosed with cannabis dependence on at least three or more study occasions had an average loss of 5.8 IQ points. After controlling for gender, nicotine use, comorbid schizophrenia, and alcohol use, they also found specific deficits in executive functioning, sustained attention, verbal list learning, and psychomotor speed associated with persistent cannabis dependence, findings that are generally consistent with cross-sectional studies.[29]

The following comes from the United States' 2012 *Proceedings of the National Academy of Sciences* (PNAS) – 'one of the world's most-cited and comprehensive multidisciplinary scientific journals'. It reports similar concerns:

Persistent cannabis use was associated with neuropsychological decline broadly across domains of functioning, even after controlling for years of education. Informants also reported noticing more cognitive problems for persistent cannabis users. Impairment was concentrated among adolescent-onset cannabis users, with more persistent use associated with greater decline. Further, cessation of cannabis use did not fully restore neuropsychological functioning among adolescent-onset cannabis users. Findings are suggestive of a neurotoxic effect of cannabis on the adolescent brain and highlight the importance of prevention and policy efforts targeting adolescents.[30]

Accumulating evidence suggests that long-term, heavy cannabis use may cause enduring neuropsychological impairment – impairment that persists beyond the period of acute intoxication. Studies of long-term, heavy cannabis users fairly consistently show that these individuals perform worse on neuropsychological tests, and some but not all studies suggest that impairment may remain even after extended periods of abstinence.[31]

Columbia University's Centre on Addiction and Substance Abuse (CASA) continues the refrain:

Smoking marijuana, in and of itself, is especially dangerous for teens. The drug can impair short term memory, ability to concentrate and motor skills at a time when these are particularly important to children developing and learning in school. Marijuana can stunt the intellectual, emotional and psychological development of adolescents.[32]

Kirsten Weir, writing for the American Psychological Association, quotes professor Susan Weiss, a research director at the National Institute on Drug Abuse (NIDA). At the time, Professor Weiss was speaking at the National Academy of Sciences in 2012. She compares the cognitive detriments of persistent marijuana use with exposure to lead:

The team found that persistent marijuana use was linked to a decline in IQ, even after the researchers controlled for educational differences. The most persistent users – those who reported using the drug in three or more waves of the study – experienced a drop in neuropsychological functioning equivalent to about six IQ points (PNAS, 2012). 'That's in the same realm as what you'd see with lead exposure,' says Weiss. 'It's not a trifle.'[33]

Such data prompted the American Psychological Association to warn about misinformation:

> It is becoming increasingly critical to publicize these research findings in any settings that serve adolescents and young adults (e.g., schools, military, mental-health clinics, medical schools, and to parents). It needs to be emphasized that regular cannabis use, defined here as once a week, is not safe and may result in addiction and neurocognitive damage, especially in youth.[34]

Scientific organizations report serious cognitive decline during and after use. These effects, even if less than reported, condemn its use. If we grasped prior notions in the Temple of the Mind – 'the human emblem', 'the confused peacock' and 'polluting parliament, sacking CERN and desecrating Darwin' – we need no extra evidence. Professionals and institutions express concern with the level of misinformation passed around by the general public. To address the issue of misinformation, I offer some final data. This information should, at least, be *considered* by those who support marijuana use.

Marijuana and mental health

At this point, we've heard that marijuana can cause neurocognitive damage. We can see – experientially and scientifically – that it reduces mental functioning. Yet darker dangers may lurk amidst cannabis' green foliage.

Broken record moment: the data might be skewed, even manufactured, but so could all data on pro-marijuana sites. I believe, however, it's important to *hear* (if not believe) what is said. So, here's the info.

The US National Institutes of Health (NIH) is comprised of many institutes. The National Institute on Drug Abuse (NIDA) is one of them. In their paper *Is There a Link Between Marijuana Use and Psychiatric Disorders?* they state:

> Several studies have linked marijuana use to increased risk for psychiatric disorders, including psychosis (schizophrenia), depression, anxiety, and substance use disorders, but whether and to what extent it actually causes these conditions is not always easy to determine. The amount of drug used, the age at first use, and genetic vulnerability have all been shown to influence this relationship. The strongest evidence to date concerns links between marijuana use and substance use disorders and between marijuana use and psychiatric disorders in those with a preexisting genetic or other vulnerability.[35]

The NIDA then reports a potential link between the AKT1 gene and psychosis:

> One study found that the risk for psychosis among those with this variant was seven times higher for daily marijuana users compared with infrequent or non-users. Marijuana use has also been shown to worsen the course of illness in patients who already have schizophrenia. As mentioned previously, marijuana can also produce an acute psychotic reaction in non-schizophrenic users, especially at high doses, although this fades as the drug wears off.

Inconsistent and modest associations have been reported between marijuana use and suicidal thoughts and attempted suicide among teens. Marijuana has also been associated with an *amotivational syndrome*, defined as a diminished or absent drive to engage in typically rewarding activities.[36]

In an update to its series of reports *Clearing the Smoke on Cannabis*, the Canadian Centre on Substance Use and Addiction continues the cautionary tale:

Chronic cannabis use has been shown to impair various cognitive abilities, such as attention, memory and decision making. For most people, these impairments are relatively mild and are reversible after a few weeks of abstinence. However, current research suggests that chronic cannabis use:

- Increases a person's risk for developing psychotic symptoms and schizophrenia when started early in life, especially among people who might have a pre-existing genetic risk;
- Increases the risk for psychosis for people who use cannabis that is high in delta-9-tetrahydrocannabinol (THC) and low in cannabidiol (CBD); and
- Is associated with other mental health conditions, such as depression and anxiety; however, the nature of this relationship is not yet clear.[37]

Regarding this, the UK's Royal College of Psychiatrists writes:

Mental health problems
There is growing evidence that people with serious mental illness, including depression and psychosis, are more likely to use cannabis or have used it for long periods of time in the past. Regular use of the drug has appeared to double the risk

of developing a psychotic episode or long-term schizophrenia. However, does cannabis cause depression and schizophrenia or do people with these disorders use it as a medication?

Over the past few years, research has strongly suggested that there is a clear link between early cannabis use and later mental health problems in those with a genetic vulnerability – and that there is a particular issue with the use of cannabis by adolescents.

Depression

A study following 1600 Australian school-children, aged 14 to 15 for seven years, found that while children who use cannabis regularly have a significantly higher risk of depression, the opposite was not the case – children who already suffered from depression were not more likely than anyone else to use cannabis. However, adolescents who used cannabis daily were five times more likely to develop depression and anxiety in later life.

Psychoses – schizophrenia and bipolar disorder

There is now sufficient evidence to show that those who use cannabis particularly at a younger age, such as around the age of 15, have a higher than average risk of developing a psychotic illness, such as schizophrenia or bipolar disorder.

These studies also show that the risk is dose-related. In other words, the more cannabis someone used, the more likely they were to develop a psychotic illness.[38]

In an online article, 'Marijuana use may be harmful to mental health', Harvard Medical School also points out potential dangers:

Think smoking marijuana is harmless? Think again. Chronic users of the drug often find themselves lacking motivation.

Some even seem depressed or have other signs of mental illness. But does chronic marijuana use lead to psychiatric problems? Or do people suffering from mental illness use marijuana to self-medicate? While this drug was becoming increasingly popular with young people in the 1990s, researchers were busy trying to figure out if marijuana was a cause or an effect of psychiatric problems. And their work seems to have paid off. Research now indicates that marijuana use increases the risk of depression, as well as schizophrenia. But at the same time, depressed people do not use marijuana more often than their non-depressed counterparts.[39]

They then report an Australian study of teenaged marijuana users:

The researchers found that the young women who had used marijuana weekly as teenagers were twice as likely to have depression as a young adult than women who did not use the drug. Daily use as a teenager was associated with four times the risk of depression for young women.

Also, among the young adults, women who used marijuana daily were five times more likely to experience depression and anxiety than those who did not use the drug. However, the researchers found no relationship between teenage depression and anxiety and later use of marijuana. This refutes the idea that youths suffering from depression turn to marijuana as a way of self-medicating.[40]

They recount another study performed in Baltimore:

The results showed people who initially did not have depressive symptoms but abused marijuana were more than four times as likely to have depressive symptoms at the follow-up date than those who did not abuse marijuana. The depressive symptoms associated with earlier marijuana abuse included suicidal thoughts and a feeling of boredom. As in the Australian study, participants with depressive symptoms at the start of the study were not more likely to abuse marijuana later on than participants without such symptoms.[41]

And another carried out in Sweden:

Marijuana use has also been linked to schizophrenia. In a study of 50,000 Swedish military draftees, the use of marijuana during adolescence was associated with a 30% increase in risk of developing schizophrenia. The study also showed a higher risk of schizophrenia with more frequent marijuana use . . .

From these studies, it is clear that marijuana use is related to subsequent depression and schizophrenia. It is still not clear, however, whether marijuana triggers the onset of illness in individuals predisposed to such conditions or whether it actually causes the illnesses. Some researchers believe that psychosocial factors that result from marijuana use – such as educational failure and unemployment – may contribute to depression. Other researchers think that marijuana may have a lasting chemical effect on the central nervous system and its functions involving memory, emotion, cognition, and movement.[42]

Harvard Medical School ends the section with concern about misinformation:

In addition to its widespread availability, marijuana's recent popularity may be largely based on the perception that it is safer than cigarettes and alcohol, according to an editorial in the *British Medical Journal*. But these studies show marijuana is not the harmless drug many believe it is, but that it can have a negative impact on your mental health.[43]

Might the National Institute on Drug Abuse, the Royal College of Psychiatrists and Harvard Medical School be lying? Yes. They might be. Do many people ignore, or remain unaware of this data? Surely, they do. Deception is disconcerting. I am more concerned, however, that most people know nothing about how marijuana may damage their health and mental health. Then they act (and misinform others) with this same deficiency of data.

Weed and the Temple of the Soul

Friends filled my living room. All afternoon, we smoked dope, giggled and engaged in silliness, dusted with pseudo-philo-sophical chitchat. Out of twelve present, eight friends had – previously and in private – shared their disdain for marijuana. They had confided that weed depleted their drive, made them sedentary, depressive, mentally slower and socially uncomfort-able. Further, they had agreed that, under its influence, they would not seek *natural* highs, that the chemical crutch atro-phied their aspirations.

Nevertheless, that afternoon, the entire group began praising weed – its joys, its pleasures, its soothing properties. I knew the majority hated marijuana's hampering effects. Still, they celebrated it – that is, sadly, how addiction plays out. My anger surged.

I had long battled addiction. I hated weed's consequences. I had spoken to eight of these friends, hoping to find support for change, for growth. They had been genuine and open. Now, they were lying – presenting a facade. I reacted inappropriately; I angrily called them on their dishonesty.

'What are you guys talking about!?' I snarled. 'You, you and you . . .' I pointed to them in turn, 'told me you hate weed. You're lying.' I continued, 'Getting highs from this stupid stick,' I held up a rolled joint, 'stops us from growing!' One of my friends spoke up, 'Whatever, Rob. I like weed. It calms me down and it's fun!'

'But that's the problem!' I cried. 'You want to be *naturally* calm, not depend on a drug. It's a crutch! You want fun, real fun, natural fun – not a drug-induced illusion.' I had – understandably – upset my friends. At this point, I *felt* there was no retreat, so I continued, 'I want be at ease, calm and peaceful – from the inside. But I want it to be *me!* I don't want a high from *nothing*. Nothing comes free. We have to grow, develop, evolve, and this crutch blocks us from doing so.' At that point, I swore, and walked out of my own house.

I acted dishonourably. I betrayed my friends' confidence, and for that I offer no excuse. Anger drove me, anger at myself, at lost potential, potentialities that would remain hidden because of a weed.

A narrative interlude: Jaunts without joints

As we've seen, many deny marijuana addiction. But if you failed to quit over a hundred times, you'd never question pot's power. My battle raged because I daily witnessed its deteriorative effects. I despised the social awkwardness weed caused. I detested the mental cloud that filled my skull under its influence, as well as the morning after – weed hangovers are horrid.

Yet I finally heaved off the habit (for a time) and began to seek peace, purpose and meaning. In my new search, I often walked in the forest, sometimes on a daily basis, experiencing nature, finding therein a solace not experienced in years. During this period, I socialized much less, trying to distance myself from prior predilections.

One day, I was leaving on a nature jaunt, when my friends Travis and Justin bumped into me. Travis asked, 'Hey Rob, where've you been lately?'

'I've been around,' I replied quickly, eager to walk my forest trails.

Justin noticed my impatience, 'Where are you going?'

I told them I was going hiking by myself. Travis' reply struck me.

'By yourself?' he said, sounding surprised, 'I could do that if I had a bag of weed with me.'

Justin started laughing, 'Yeah. No kidding!'

I sighed and said, 'That's sad, you guys. You can't enjoy nature without drugs.'

Justin piped up, 'No way. You gotta have a couple joints if you're going hiking.'

I'll never forget Travis' face, his mouth slightly open, eyes introspective, a disturbed and confused look spreading across his face.

'No. Rob's right. It is sad.' He spoke distantly, 'Oh God, I can't even enjoy walking in a forest without drugs.'

I found this chilling, and still do.

Anything chemicals offer exists within us – in pure (and actual) form. The crutch atrophies the attribute, withers the will, and weakens our capacities. In the end, innate abilities remain inactive, whittled away by a noxious weed.

The Temple of the Heart wails at weed

The Temple of the Heart (not yet mentioned) demands we drop dope and work for a better world. If we support a chemical culture, we allow real life – a life of knowledge, service and love – to pass by in silence and stupor. Love for human potential summons us to abandon all chemical pastimes. How can a heart be at peace if we disfigure what it naturally loves? The Temple of the Heart wails because weed vandalizes its sister Temples: Body, Mind and Soul.

A mini bottom bar

The Temples convict weed of vandalism. Marijuana – like all chemical pastimes – defaces these noble edifices. Our innate capacities are deeper than any drug, more precious than any gem. And these gems – illusorily offered by marijuana – lie within the unhewn rock of our current selves; we must dig them out. To cling to a chemical crutch because it's less deleterious is foolish. Humankind must cast off this excess baggage to scale heights yet unseen.

Encourage those unaided by chemical crutches. Support them in their search for sober thought, and hence, personal and social evolution. This is the path of a true friend, and the path of a warrior.

8

Warriors of Light

It follows that all who work for the Supreme Design are soldiers in the army of the Spirit . . .

The light of the celestial world makes war against the world
of shadow and illusion. The rays of the Sun of Truth dispel
the darkness of superstition and misunderstanding.[1]

An uncomfortable metaphor

The Faith of God, the 'Supreme Design', summons us to 'make
war against the world of shadow and illusion' – a stirring vision
for some; for others, a source of unease.

In our day, 'the warrior' elicits anxiety, especially in a religious context. Understandably, people associate religion with
violence, an association forged by conflicts between (and within)
faith communities, as well as our fixation on the graphic, the
lewd, the shocking.

Nevertheless, warrior symbolism resonates with deep-seated
yearning: the longing to fight for the good, the true, the just and
the beautiful. We need a serious, intelligent renaissance of the
spiritual warrior symbol – one who battles for light, love and
mercy, whose weapons are not tanks but tongues, not planes
but pens.

The warrior forfeits self-interest, sacrifices desire and comfort – even life – for the community's preservation and progress. The Bahá'í Writings – as with all Scriptures – employ warrior symbols, summoning us to rise up, undaunted and unflinching, to battle for love, peace and justice. As a Bahá'í, I recognize that the soul, to be properly awakened, requires such symbols. Why would I think this? . . . All Manifestations of God use the battle cry to summon humanity to peace – a difficult task, no doubt.

Surely, harmonious nature images flood Bahá'í Scripture. The Bahá'í Faith's Central Figures refer to humans as birds of one flock, flowers of one garden, as waves of one sea. We hear of doves, gazelles, nightingales, stars, suns and breezes. Poetic symbols dwell on every page of Bahá'í Scripture. Yet we also find numerous quotations calling us warriors, soldiers fighting for world unity.

Bahá'í warriors don't focus, however, on the battle against chemical dependence – more vital fronts command our attention. Yet the warrior-call does summon us to cast away ephemeral pursuits in the quest for grander goals. Bahá'u'lláh sounds His trumpet:

Subdue the citadels of men's hearts with the swords of wisdom and of utterance . . . The sword of wisdom is hotter than summer heat, and sharper than blades of steel, if ye do but understand.[2]

Set your reliance on the army of justice, put on the armour of wisdom, let your adorning be forgiveness and mercy and that which cheereth the hearts of the well-favoured of God.[3]

'Abdu'l-Bahá repeats the refrain:

The triumphant hosts of the Celestial Concourse, arrayed and marshalled in the Realms above, stand ready and expectant to

assist and assure victory to that valiant horseman who with
confidence spurs on his charger into the arena of service. Well
is it with that fearless warrior, who armed with the power of
true Knowledge, hastens unto the field, disperses the armies
of ignorance, and scatters the hosts of error, who holds aloft
the Standard of Divine Guidance, and sounds the Clarion of
Victory.[4]

O ye beloved of the Lord! This day is the day of union, the
day of the ingathering of all mankind. 'Verily God loveth
those who, as though they were a solid wall, do battle for
His Cause in serried lines!' Note that He saith 'in serried
lines'– meaning crowded and pressed together, one locked to
the next, each supporting his fellows. To do battle, as stated
in the sacred verse, doth not, in this greatest of all dispen-
sations, mean to go forth with sword and spear, with lance
and piercing arrow – but rather weaponed with pure intent,
with righteous motives, with counsels helpful and effective,
with godly attributes, with deeds pleasing to the Almighty,
with the qualities of heaven. It signifieth education for all
mankind, guidance for all men, the spreading far and wide
of the sweet savours of the spirit, the promulgation of God's
proofs, the setting forth of arguments conclusive and divine,
the doing of charitable deeds.[5]

Such images stir my soul. 'Abdu'l-Bahá calls us to be 'valiant
horsemen', 'fearless warriors', to charge 'into the arena of service', 'armed with the power of true Knowledge', disperse
'the armies of ignorance', and scatter 'the hosts of error'. They
summon us to do battle 'in serried lines' with the weapons of
'pure intent', offering our counsels, 'setting forth . . . arguments
conclusive and divine'.
    Shoghi Effendi, the Guardian of the Bahá'í Faith, offers the

following exhortation. For clarity of focus, I have added the emphasis in *italics:*

> The individual alone must assess its character, consult his conscience, prayerfully consider all its aspects, manfully struggle against the natural inertia that weighs him down in his effort to arise, *shed, heroically and irrevocably, the trivial and superfluous attachments which hold him back. . .*
>
> The gross materialism that engulfs the entire nation at the present hour; *the attachment to worldly things that enshrouds the souls of men*; the fears and anxieties that distract their minds; *the pleasure and dissipations that fill their time*, the prejudices and animosities that darken their outlook, *the apathy and lethargy that paralyze their spiritual faculties* – these are among the formidable obstacles that *stand in the path of every would-be warrior in the service of Bahá'u'lláh*, obstacles which he *must battle against and surmount in his crusade for the redemption of his own countrymen. . .*
>
> Delicate and *strenuous though the task may be, however arduous and prolonged the effort required, whatsoever the nature of the perils and pitfalls* that beset the path of whoever arises to revive the fortunes of a Faith *struggling against the rising forces of materialism, nationalism, secularism, racialism, ecclesiasticism*, the all-conquering potency of the grace of God, vouchsafed through the Revelation of Bahá'u'lláh, will, undoubtedly, mysteriously and surprisingly, *enable whosoever arises to champion His Cause to win complete and total victory.*[6]

Every 'would-be warrior' will confront 'formidable obstacles' in this path. Yet, 'emptied of self' we must 'combat the forces' arrayed against us. Eyes open to humanity's suffering, our hearts well-tilled, a surge of responsibility, an upwelling of urgency shall seize us, stirring us to rise up, sacrifice our petty desires and fight for humanity's 'redemption'. Our culture's chemical affections epitomize these 'trivial and superfluous attachments' that distract our minds, and 'paralyze' our 'spiritual faculties' – smearing the Temples of Body, Heart, Mind and Soul.

For well-nigh two centuries, the Bahá'í community has invited peoples of all Faiths, communities and creeds to work together to combat 'the rising forces of materialism, nationalism, secularism, racialism, ecclesiasticism'. Bahá'í or not, we need warriors – armed with pure deeds and wise counsel – to heal and regenerate our world; it sorely needs it. As well, Bahá'í or not, we believe the forces of light support and sustain all those who serve the cause of unity and love, who serve the Good, the True and the Beautiful.

Faced with such a vital, yet herculean task, no warrior would contemplate weakening themselves with chemical crutches and deleterious distractions. Rather, they would cast aside such hindrances and heed a calling such as this:

> O ye loved ones of God! In this, the Bahá'í dispensation, God's Cause is spirit unalloyed. His Cause belongeth not to the material world. It cometh neither for strife nor war, nor for acts of mischief or of shame; it is neither for quarrelling with other Faiths, nor for conflicts with the nations. Its only army is the love of God, its only joy the clear wine of His knowledge, its only battle the expounding of the Truth; its one crusade is against the insistent self, the evil promptings of the human heart. Its victory is to submit and yield, and to be selfless is its everlasting glory.[7]

Self-esteem and the warrior: You can't love yourself until you love others

On this path, we need self-confidence, self-esteem and self-respect – goals all humans seek. Yet we seek where they cannot be found. Distracted and off course, therefore, we construct our citadels of self-esteem on a sinking marsh.

To explain, imagine the following:

> You live in a village where everyone depends on neighbours for support in hard times. One day, you are playing cards in your basement, relaxing with friends at the end of a long week. Suddenly, a clamour erupts outside. You hear yelling, people rushing, voices serious and urgent. Then, shrieks split the air. The basement door crashes open. Your neighbor bursts in, his eyes scanning for intruders, his clothing torn, blood trailing from matted hair, an axe in his hand.
>
> 'We're under attack! They're sacking the village!'
>
> You glance at your friends, take a deep breath, and nod your head. They nod in reply. And so, you leap to your feet, grab your neighbour's arm, drag him to the door, push him out, and slam it shut.
>
> Then you march back to the table, sit down and say, 'So guys, you in for another game? Good! Whose deal is it?'

A bizarre story, you think? Who would respond so coldly, abandoning neighbours in crisis? But what if you could barricade the door and had ample food stockpiled? What if you could ride out the assault? Far more likely then, isn't it?

The point is this: having forsaken your community, how could you respect yourself? Any semblance of self-respect would be mere self-deception. Yet, most of us – including myself – metaphorically play cards while people destroy actual villages.

I feel deeply uneasy pointing this out, but I believe it necessary. We must face existence, reflect with *Mind*, empathize with *Heart*, muster the *Soul*, then force the *Body* to act. Aligning heart, mind, body and soul cannot occur unless truthfulness takes centre stage.

> Truthfulness is the foundation of all human virtues. Without truthfulness progress and success, in all the worlds of God, are impossible for any soul. When this holy attribute is established in man, all the divine qualities will also be acquired.[8]

I worry because we often flee reality into the cave of denial. I worry, as well, that I will offend or upset. This is not my intention. I do hope to awaken myself and my brothers and sisters to what we can and must do to save humanity. I also hope to offer the only road to genuine self-esteem and self-confidence – one I need help walking. Fellow travellers ease weariness, fear and self-doubt.

You see, we do not live in the Middle Ages, confined to isolated hamlets. We know well our planet's plight. We're painfully aware of humanity's suffering – it's everywhere – and we *can* help. Often though, the world suffers while we play cards.

And if our global village is being sacked, and we play cards, how can we develop any deep-seated self-esteem, self-confidence or self-respect? Whatever the village's border, if we barricade our hearts and minds we build our house of self-esteem from those same cards. If we seek self-esteem, if we desire self-respect, we must serve.

Mankind's misery keeps us in our mental and emotional basements, amusing ourselves with ephemeral pastimes. Such diversions distract us while we sanction suffering – the village pillaged by paltry pursuits. Of course, I empathize with the response. How could I not? I do it daily. I understand why we drown out the midnight sighing of millions; we care – ironic as that sounds.

Yet during the attack, when everyone needs us most, we blunt (or worse, throw away) our finest weapons – our hearts, our minds, our souls. And, heedless to sorrow, forgetful of nobility, careless of clear thought, we abandon the warrior's path, and lose our self-worth.

> O Son of Man! Wert thou to speed through the immensity of space and traverse the expanse of heaven, yet thou wouldst find no rest save in submission to Our command and humbleness before Our Face.[9]

Hitting the clubs: An uncomfortable quote

In a chemical culture, celebration without substances seems strange. Hence, a youth who avoids clubs and bars can shock people. How do you socialize? Drinking and dancing often dominate the social scene, and most won't boogie without the booze.

This topic causes discomfort. We must, nevertheless, question our support of establishments reared as *Anti-Temples*: bars and clubs. To be frank, the Guardian, Shoghi Effendi, asks us to avoid the atmosphere that is so often associated with them:

> In the teachings there is nothing against dancing, but the friends should remember that the standard of Bahá'u'lláh is modesty and chastity. The atmosphere of modern dance halls, where so much smoking and drinking and promiscuity goes on, is very bad, but decent dances are not harmful in themselves. There is certainly no harm in classical dancing or learning dancing in school. There is also no harm in taking part in dramas. Likewise in cinema acting. The harmful thing,

nowadays, is not the art itself but the unfortunate corruption which often surrounds these arts. As Bahá'ís we need avoid none of the arts, but acts and the atmosphere that sometimes go with these professions we should avoid.[10]

This quotation can elicit strong reactions from young adults. 'That's what people our age do!' or 'You'd oust yourself from the social scene!' How do you avoid clubs when peers so often frequent them? The test is real, no doubt. But what is the option?

Be strong, be a leader, be a warrior. Frankly, we either lead society or it leads us; we have to choose. When we indulge in the club atmosphere, we no longer stand apart from our declining age, an age so lost and confused. Rather, we *appear* to condone the practices; most mistake us as partakers. And though we may not partake, we certainly enable. We support these establishments and offer no alternative.

In the Bahá'í Writings, worship includes the arts: music, poetry, dance, drama, painting. We pray when we engage in these beautiful practices. Even more, we can elevate hearts and minds, create joyful atmospheres, and craft social spaces congruent with our potential. We can exalt humanity, and do it without chemical crutches that diminish our dignity and atrophy our spirits and bodies.

We are spiritual beings. Thus, we yearn for arts free from substances that erode the bodies, hearts and the minds that perform them. In short, create venues where people can do this. Offer alternate paths. Let us show how things *can* and *should* be! If this appears too ambitious, find events that already exist and support them!

9

The Homecoming Clean

Rebellion redefined

At the tour's start, I spoke about rebellious sheep. How ironic it is – in a dominantly drug-using culture – to accuse an abstainer of 'conforming'. Maybe, being a rebel – in some age – meant partying all the time, drinking booze, taking drugs, and being indifferent to important matters: being cool. If it ever lived, this rebellion is long dead.

I believe that now, to rebel you should be educated, abundantly virtuous, and care deeply for humanity. To stand for justice, clarity, community and compassion in the face of apathy and lethargy – this is rebellion.

We must redefine 'rebellion' and channel the impulse towards its white lily, instead of 'wandering distracted' in a sordid swamp. We should rebel, that part is clear. We should rebel against injustice, hatred, indolence, irrationality, prejudice – all brutish instincts. If youth (or anyone) seek distinction, they should serve humanity, not be served booze. Abstinence, calm deliberation, eloquence, chastity, detachment, empathy, sacrifice and deep thought define the revolutionary, not sheep-like party behaviour and materialistic longings.

Abstaining from 'abstinence'

Another term begs for redefinition. All along, I've used the term 'abstinence'. But I find it imprecise and misleading. It plays into pub propaganda, suggesting that sobriety is a form of holding back: abstaining. It implies that I yearn for chemical pastimes, but pull back, like a rider reining in a wild steed longing to be free. Yet I view my choice in more positive terms.

I don't abstain from alcohol any more than I abstain from heroin. Simply, I don't wish to debase my mind by injecting addictive chemicals into my bloodstream. I don't abstain from cock-fights; I find pitting roosters (or any animal) against each other in death matches horrid. Sorry, but again, I don't *abstain* from prostitution. Rather, I don't *want* to rent humans for sordid sense-gratification. I believe the sex trade to be grotesque, even more so when filmed – pornography. Recall my mundane examples from *Vindicating vulgarity?* I don't curb my desire to leave food in my teeth. I don't hold back from leaving pasta stains on my shirt, don't reign myself in lest I break free and sport noticeable nasal mucus. I would never think of doing so.

I don't abstain from alcohol and drugs. I don't hold back. I go forward and stand for clarity, rational thought, a healthy body, and empathic concern for my fellow humans. I stand for the human psyche's freedom, independence from chemical crutches, and reverence for heart and mind. Obviously, I think everyone else should as well. Many see this way forward to greater freedom and harmony, and yet choose to abstain.

A revealing retort: Why not live a little?

People accuse me of being too serious. They propose I 'lighten up', be less burdened by the world. I find this odd, mainly because I am not a gloomy person. Though it may not come through in my writing, I joke regularly, act like a clown, carry innocent witticisms too far, and laugh frequently – mostly at my own silly little jokes.

'Abdu'l-Bahá tells us:

> Joy gives us wings! In times of joy our strength is more vital, our intellect keener, and our understanding less clouded. We seem better able to cope with the world and to find our sphere of usefulness.[1]

Humour delights the spirit. Happiness releases our abilities. We should explore and develop our capacity for joy, humour, a lightness of spirit. At the same time, humanity sorely needs a well-directed sense of gravity.

In context, the accusation of seriousness means I should drink, at least a little. However, people accuse me of being over-serious when I speak on humanity's suffering. The allegation roams even wider. I've heard it when I speak about history, science, philosophy, and of course, religion. When accused of 'seriousness' I (once again) question the definition. The term, as commonly used, hides a bias.

Everyone is serious about something. Obviously, I am included. But the question can't be whether or not we should *ever* be serious. Rather: 'What *should* we be serious about?' All people – including the self-identified 'carefree' – believe matters of import exist; anyone who values anything will.

For example, I observe the 'care-free' often quite serious about television or sports. I've been described as serious by people deeply concerned with money or physical appearances. I've had individuals claim I fixate on global issues to excess, only to watch them ensure they have the latest celebrity magazine. I've had those who call me solemn debate – heatedly – the best sports team, actor, martial art, musician, brand of whisky or fast-food chain. I hear acquaintances express passion for video games, cellphones, cars or computers, sports events, even soap operas – the list goes on.

I could echo: 'Don't be so serious! You only live once. Go learn, master your mind, train your body, study the arts, and serve your community. Seek purpose and meaning. Explore philosophy. Delve into social activism. Don't be so serious about sports, television, work, cars, clothes, tech gadgets . . .'

Our culture displays constant seriousness in odd ways, in odd areas. People don't lack seriousness or a sense of import; it's misdirected.

Years ago, a coworker asked why I seemed frustrated. I replied frankly, 'Human suffering disturbs me. I'm upset by child exploitation – for labour, sex and war. I think of the wars raging, malnutrition, child poverty, curable diseases . . .' I sighed.

He looked startled and said, 'Rob, you can't let that stuff bother you.'

I took a deep breath and looked at him intently. 'Would you have said that if I told you I got cut off on the freeway, or that someone stole my cellphone, that I blew a tire or forgot to record my favourite TV show? Or, would you have empathized, and said, "Ya. I know what you mean. I hate when that happens"'?

Wonderfully, he paused, smiled, and said, 'Well, yes, I would have. Isn't that bizarre!' He went on, 'We empathize with meaningless and passing problems, but genuine concern for humanity, we find *that* odd. Sorry Rob, I'll never do that again.' We are now good friends.

The final point and the bottom-est bar

Millions die yearly from war, famine, and disease. Racial, religious and political tensions whip the world into feral states. The globe spends hundreds of billions on weapons. Children work in sweat-shops. Mere youth pick up firearms. The world longs for guidance in a dark night.

Given humanity's state, we can't honestly wonder if ingesting intellect-draining chemicals is appropriate, let alone progressive. We must unite the planet, raise consciousness, ennoble ourselves and others, establish universal education, evolve our political systems, and alleviate the suffering of billions. Recognizing this, is ingesting injurious chemicals a worthy endeavour? The question seems absurd. We could unite the races, eradicate abject poverty, enable people to feel loved, precious and whole. Why pause to weigh the merits of downing mind-depleting liquids? As I asked at the beginning: Do you think an ever-advancing civilization – guided by forbearance, mercy and compassion, dedicated to the pursuit of progress and nobility – would cling to alcohol and drug use?

The only answer: a definitive 'No'. Chemical pastimes damage the Temple of the Body, harm the Temple of the Heart, desecrate the Temple of the Mind, and atrophy the Temple of the Soul. They deteriorate what's finest in humanity – what makes us human. But I think (somewhere inside) we knew this all along.

In this culture, sobriety is socially difficult. Being a healthy-loving-soulful-rationalist (now that's a mouthful) is at best misunderstood, at worst a character flaw. People perceive sobriety as puritanically avoiding an obvious accoutrement to the good life. Some view sobriety with confusion, pity or even disdain.

I hope I have calmed the confusion, transformed disdain (at least) into silent admiration, and turned the tables on pity, for a caged tiger, or a flightless eagle (even a *confused peacock*) can elicit no other response.

I want ferocious felines, stunning peacocks, shimmering

gold – healthy, sacrificial, insightful and virtuous humans. To achieve this, we must share these values with others. This proves challenging. Therefore, I offer this passage from the Bahá'í supreme governing body: the Universal House of Justice:

> In one of His Tablets Bahá'u'lláh warns the Bahá'ís: 'Dispute not with any one concerning the things of this world and its affairs, for God hath abandoned them to such as have set their affection upon them. Out of the whole world He hath chosen for Himself the hearts of men – hearts which the hosts of revelation and of utterance can subdue.' (*Gleanings* CXX-VIII) As you realize, this cannot mean that Bahá'ís must not be controversial since, in many societies, being a Bahá'í is itself a controversial matter.[2]

To be a Bahá'í is, in many ways, to be controversial. Surely, this doesn't mean being crude, belligerent or contentious. We must be considerate, well-spoken, noble and loyal to grand goals. This, however, generates disagreement. Controversy surfaces because we call into question long-entrenched values, revered ideas and treasured traditions. We cannot avoid this, nor the inescapable storm it will engender. And our controversial nature manifests on numerous fronts.

Bahá'ís stand for racial and religious unity, gender equality, a spiritual economy, global governance, ending dire poverty and opulent wealth, universal education, the harmony of religion and science, and yes, freedom from chemical crutches. We must be loving, articulate, idealistic, pure in motive, compassionate and kind, but this will not avoid controversy; it is controversial to be so.

From tourist to pilgrim: An invitation

Dear friends, we've completed our tour of Temples dedicated to the Body, Heart, Mind and Soul. We've parted the veil of normalcy, tended rebellious sheep, visited confused peacocks, and cleansed our mental shirts of symbolic pasta stains. On our journey, we've sought lilies in the swamps, dodged will-o-the wisps, avoided mirages, followed Ulysses to the lotus-eaters' island, and asked 'What about the weed?' We've envisioned a manure-stained CERN, a polluted parliament, and a Darwinian book-burning. We've met warriors, cowardly card-players, and questioned definitions of *freedom, abstinence* and *rebellion.*

I feel honoured to have been your guide, thankful for your patience, and grateful for your willingness to overlook my shortcomings and – at times – overly passionate pleas. I hope you will invite others to tour these Temples.

And now, having visited these noble edifices, I hope you return as admirer, as lover – no longer as tourist, but rather as a pilgrim.

Bibliography

'Abdu'l-Bahá. *Paris Talks: Addresses given by 'Abdu'l-Bahá in 1911* (1912). London: Bahá'í Publishing Trust, 12th ed. 1995.

— *The Promulgation of Universal Peace: Talks Delivered by 'Abdu'l-Bahá During His Visit to the United States and Canada in 1912* (1922, 1925). Comp. H. MacNutt. Wilmette, IL: Bahá'í Publishing Trust, rev. ed. 2012.

— *Selections from the Writings of 'Abdu'l-Bahá.* Comp. Research Department of the Universal House of Justice. Haifa: Bahá'í World Centre, 1978.

American Heart Association (AHA), 'Alcohol and heart health', online article, updated 12 January 2015. http://www.heart.org/HEARTORG/Conditions/More/MyHeartandStrokeNews/Alcohol-and-Heart-Disease_UCM_305173_Article.jsp.

American Psychological Association. 'Regular marijuana use bad for teens' brains: Psychology and public health experts weigh in on potential effects of legalization on youth', press release 9 August 2014. http://www.apa.org/news/press/releases/2014/08/regular-marijuana.aspx.

Anderson, Peter; Baumberg, Ben. *Alcohol in Europe: A Public Health Perspective*, report for the European Commission. London: Institute of Alcohol Studies, 2006. http://btg.ias.org.uk/pdfs/alcohol-in-europe/alcohol-ineu_full_en.pdf.

Ashton, C. Heather. 'Pharmacology and effects of cannabis: A brief review', in *The British Journal of Psychiatry*, vol. 178, no. 2 (Feb. 2001). http://bjp.rcpsych.org/content/178/2/101?ijkey=dcb86ada11426db047baccbd67b5b228a9514c82&keytype2=tf_ipsecsha#sec-6.

Bahá'í Reference Library. Authoritative online source of Bahá'í writings. https://www.bahai.org/library/.

Bahá'í World Centre. *One Common Faith.* Haifa: Bahá'í World Centre, 2005.

Bahá'u'lláh. *The Call of the Divine Beloved: Selected Mystical Works of Bahá'u'lláh.* Haifa, Bahá'í World Centre, 2018.

— *Epistle to the Son of the Wolf.* Trans. Shoghi Effendi. Wilmette, IL: Bahá'í Publishing Trust, rev. ed. 1976.

— *Gleanings from the Writings of Bahá'u'lláh.* Trans. Shoghi Effendi. Wilmette, IL: Bahá'í Publishing Trust, 2nd ed. 1976.

— *The Hidden Words of Bahá'u'lláh.* Trans. Shoghi Effendi. Wilmette, IL: Bahá'í Publishing Trust, 1970; New Delhi: Bahá'í Publishing Trust, 1987.

— *The Kitáb-i-Aqdas: The Most Holy Book.* Haifa: Bahá'í World Centre, 1992.

— *Tablets of Bahá'u'lláh Revealed After the Kitáb-i-Aqdas.* Comp. Research Department of the Universal House of Justice. Haifa: Bahá'í World Centre, 1978.

Benson, B. L. ; Rasmussen, D. W. ; Zimmerman, P. R. *The Impact of Alcohol Control Policies on the Incidence of Violent Crime*, report submitted to the National Criminal Justice Reference Service – US Department of Justice, summary in *NIJ Journal*, no. 249 (July 2003). https://www.ncjrs.gov/pdffiles1/jr000249f.pdf.

Bunge, Valerie Pottie; Johnson, Holly; Baldé, Thierno A. *Exploring Crime Patterns in Canada*, Crime and Justice Research Paper Series, Canadian Centre for Justice Statistics and Time Series Research and Analysis Centre. Ottawa: Statistics Canada, 2005. http://www.publications.gc.ca/Collection/Statcan/85-561-MIE/85-561-MIE2005005.pdf.

'Cannabis/Marijuana', online article in *Psychology Today*. https://www.psychologytoday.com/conditions/cannabismarijuana.

Canadian Centre on Substance Abuse. 'Canadian drug summary' online article, August 2014. http://www.ccsa.ca/Resource%20Library/CCSA-Canadian-Drug-Summary-Alcohol-2014-en.pdf.

— '*Clearing the Smoke on Cannabis: Highlights – An update*', online article. http://www.ccdus.ca/Eng/topics/Cannabis/Health-Impacts-of-Cannabis/Pages/default.aspx.

— *Proportions of Crimes Associated with Alcohol and Other Drugs in Canada.* Toronto: Canadian Centre on Substance Abuse, 2002. http://www.ccsa. ca/Resource%20Library/ccsa-009105-2002.pdf.

Centers for Disease Control and Prevention (CDC). 'Marijuana: How can it affect your health?', online article. https://www.cdc.gov/marijuana/ health-effects.html.

Centre for Addiction and Mental Health (CAMH). *Alcohol and Chronic Health Problems.* Toronto: CAMH, 2012. http://www.camh.ca/en/ education/about/camh_publications/Documents/Flat_PDFs/alcohol_ chronic_health.pdf.

Crean, Rebecca D. et al. 'An evidence based review of acute and long-term effects of cannabis use on executive cognitive functions', in *Journal of Addiction Medicine*, vol. 5, no. 1 (2011), pp. 1–8. https://www.ncbi.nlm. nih.gov/pmc/articles/PMC3037578/.

Grinspoon, Peter. 'Medical marijuana', Harvard Health Blog, Harvard Medical School (Harvard Health Publications), 15 Jan. 2018. http://www. health.harvard.edu/mind-and-mood/medical-marijuana-and-the-mind.

Gupta, Bina (ed.). *Ethical Questions: East and West.* New York and Oxford: Rowman & Littlefield, 2002.

Harvard Medical School (Harvard Health Publications). 'Marijuana use may be harmful to mental health: The Family HealthGuide', online article, May 2003. Originally published in *British Medical Journal*, November 2002 and *American Journal of Psychiatry*, December 2001. http://www. health.harvard.edu/mind-and-mood/marijuana-use-may-be-harmful-to- mental-health-the-family-healthguide.

Harvard School of Public Health, 'Alcohol: Balancing risks and benefits', online article in *The Nutrition Source*. http://www.hsph.harvard.edu/nu- tritionsource/alcohol-full-story.

Hathaway, Bill. 'Study links genes to marijuana dependence and major depres- sion', in *Yale News*, 30 March 2016. http://news.yale.edu/2016/03/30/ study-links-genes-marijuana-dependence-and-major-depression.

Herbert, Frank. *Chapterhouse: Dune.* New York: Ace Books, 1987.

Her Majesty's Government, Home Office (United Kingdom). *The Govern- ment's Alcohol Strategy*, document no. Cm 8336. London: Alcohol and Drugs Unit, 2012. https://www.gov.uk/government/uploads/system/up- loads/attachment_data/file/224075/alcohol-strategy.pdf.

Homer, *The Odyssey*. Trans. Samuel Butler (1900). Book IX. Online at Pagebypagebooks.com. http://www.pagebypagebooks.com/Homer_Butler_Tr/The_Odyssey/Book_IX_p2.html.

Jacobs, Bob; NASA. *NASA Acting Administrator Statement on Fiscal Year 2018 Budget Proposal* (16 March 1917). https://www.nasa.gov/press-release/nasa-acting-administrator-statement-on-fiscal-year-2018-budget-proposal.

Jernigan, David H. *Global Status Report: Alcohol and Young People*. Geneva, World Health Organization, 2001. http://whqlibdoc.who.int/hq/2001/WHO_MSD_MSB_01.1.pdf.

Johns, Andrew. 'Psychiatric effects of cannabis', in *The British Journal of Psychiatry*, vol. 178, no. 2 (Feb. 2001), pp. 116–122. http://bjp.rcpsych.org/content/178/2/116.

Lisdahl, Krista M. et al. 'Considering cannabis: The effects of regular cannabis use on neurocognition in adolescents and young adults', in *Current Addiction Reports*, vol. 1, no. 2 (June 2014), pp. 144–156. https://link.springer.com/journal/40429/1/2.

Living the Life

Mayo Clinic. 'Alcohol: If you drink keep it moderate: Moderate alcohol use has possible health benefits, but it's not risk-free', online article, 6 November 2018. http://www.mayoclinic.com/health/alcohol/SC00024.

— 'What are the benefits of CBD – and is it safe to use?', online article. https://www.mayoclinic.org/healthy-lifestyle/consumer-health/expert-answers/is-cbd-safe-and-effective/faq-20446700.

McCracken, Katie et al. *Evaluation of Alcohol Arrest Referral Pilot Schemes (Phase 2)*, Occasional Paper 102. London: Her Majesty's Government, Home Office, 2012. https://www.gov.uk/government/uploads/system/uploads/attachment_data/file/116267/occ102.pdf.

Meier, Madeline H. et al. 'Persistent cannabis users show neuropsychological decline from childhood to midlife', in *Proceedings of the National Academy of Sciences (PNAS)*. Published online 27 August 2012. http://www.pnas.org/content/109/40/E2657.full.pdf.

National Centre on Addiction and Substance Abuse (CASA). *Non-Medical Marijuana: Rite of Passage or Russian Roulette?*, White paper. New York: Columbia University, 1999. http://www.centeronaddiction.org/addiction-research/reports/non-medical-marijuana-rite-passage-or-russian-roulette.

National Criminal Justice Reference Service, US Department of Justice. 'Alcohol control policies and violent crime', in *NIJ Journal*, no. 249 (July 2003). https://www.ncjrs.gov/pdffiles1/jr000249f.pdf.

National Institute on Alcohol Abuse and Alcoholism, National Institutes of Health (NIH). 'Economic costs of alcohol and drug abuse estimated at $246 billion in the United States', news release 13 May 1998. .http://www.niaaa.nih.gov/news-events/news-releases/economic-costs-alcohol-and-drug-abuse-estimated-246-billion-united-states.

National Institute on Drug Abuse. 'Marijuana as medicine: What is medical marijuana?', online article. https://www.drugabuse.gov/publications/drugfacts/marijuana-medicine.

National Institute on Drug Abuse (NIDA), National Institutes of Health (NIH). *Is There a Link Between Marijuana Use and Psychiatric Disorders?*, Marijuana Research Report Series. Washington DC: US Department of Health and Human Services, 2016. https://www.drugabuse.gov/publications/research-reports/marijuana. Updated January 2017. https://www.drugabuse.gov/publications/marijuana/there-link-between-marijuana-use-psychiatric-disorders.

Royal College of General Practitioners. 'Cannabis and the general practitioner – Going to Pot', online article. https://www.rcgp.org.uk/policy/rcgp-policy-areas/cannabis-and-the-general-practitioner-going-to-pot.aspx.

Royal College of Psychiatrists, Public Education Editorial Board. 'Cannabis and mental health', online article, June 2014. http://www.rcpsych.ac.uk/healthadvice/problemsdisorders/cannabis.aspx.

Shoghi Effendi. *The Advent of Divine Justice* (1939). Wilmette, IL: Bahá'í Publishing Trust, 1984.

— *Citadel of Faith: Messages to America, 1947–1957*. Wilmette, IL: Bahá'í Publishing Trust, 1965.

— *Dawn of a New Day: Messages to India 1923–1957*. New Delhi: Bahá'í Publishing Trust, n.d.

— *Unfolding Destiny: The Messages from the Guardian of the Bahá'í Faith to the Bahá'í Community of the British Isles*. London: Bahá'í Publishing Trust, 1981.

Shrivastava, Amresh et al. 'Cannabis use and cognitive dysfunction', in *Indian Journal of Psychiatry*, vol. 53, no. 3 (2011), pp. 187–91. https://www.ncbi.nlm.nih.gov/pmc/articles/PMC3221171/.

United Nations Children's Fund (UNICEF). *Annual Report 2015*. New York: UNICEF, 2015. https://www.unicef.org/publications/files/UNICEF_Annual_Report_2015_En.pdf.

Universal House of Justice, The. *Messages from the Universal House of Justice 1963–1986: The Third Epoch of the Formative Age*. Comp. Geoffry W. Marks. Wilmette, IL: Bahá'í Publishing Trust, 1996.

University of California, Berkeley, School of Public Health, 'Alcohol: What moderation means', online article in *Berkeley Wellness*, 7 March 2013. http://www.berkeleywellness.com/healthy-eating/food/article/alcohol-what-moderation-means.

US Department of Health and Human Services, Public Health Service. *Substance Abuse Treatment and Domestic Violence,* Treatment Improvement Protocol (TIP) Series 25. Rockville, MD: Substance Abuse and Mental Health Services Administration (SAMHSA), rev. ed. 2012. https://www.ncbi.nlm.nih.gov/books/NBK64437/pdf/Bookshelf_NBK64437.pdf.

Weir, Kirsten. 'Marijuana and the developing brain: More states are legalizing marijuana, but concerns remain about its long-term effects on the adolescent brain', in *Monitor on Psychology* (American Psychiatric Association), vol. 46, no. 10 (Nov. 2015), p. 48. http://www.apa.org/monitor/2015/11/marijuana-brain.aspx.

World Bank. *World Development Indicators Database*. Washington DC. http://data.worldbank.org/data-catalog/world-development-indicators#.

World Food Programme (WFP). 'Contributions to WFP in 2016' (as of 26 March 2017). http://www.wfp.org/funding/year/2016.

— 'Overview', online article. http://www1.wfp.org/overview.

World Health Organization (WHO). *Alcohol and Injuries: Emergency Department Studies in an International Perspective*. Geneva: WHO, 2009. http://www.who.int/substance_abuse/msbalcinuries.pdf.

— 'Alcohol: Key facts', online article updated January 2015. http://www.who.int/mediacentre/factsheets/fs349/en/.

— *Cannabis: A Health Perspective and Research Agenda*. Geneva: WHO, 1996. http://www.who.int/iris/handle/10665/63691.

— *Global Status Report on Alcohol and Health.* Geneva: WHO, 2011. http://www.who.int/substance_abuse/publications/global_alcohol_report/msbgsruprofiles.pdf.

— Programme Budget 2016–2017. Geneva: WHO, 2016. http://www.who.int/about/finances-accountability/budget/PB201617_en.pdf?ua=1.

WorkSafeBC, *Occupational First Aid: A Reference and Training Manual.* Vancouver, BC: WorkSafeBC, 2010.

Notes and References

1. Packing Our Bags

1   Letter on behalf of Shoghi Effendi to an individual, 17 October 1944, in Shoghi Effendi, *Unfolding Destiny*, pp. 440–41.
2   Bahá'u'lláh, *Gleanings from the Writings of Bahá'u'lláh*, CXXV, p. 264.
3   Letter on behalf of the Universal House of Justice to an individual, 9 May 2015, in *Bahá'í Library Online*. https://bahai-library.com/uhj_attitude_changes_homosexuality.
4   Letter on behalf of Shoghi Effendi to an individual, 12 May 1925, in *Living the Life*, pp. 2–3; also in *Lights of Guidance*, no. 318, p. 92.
5   'Abdu'l-Bahá, *The Promulgation of Universal Peace*, p. 86.
6   ibid. pp. 265–6.

2. The Temple of the Body

1   'Abdu'l-Bahá. *Selections from the Writings of Abdu'l-Bahá*, no. 129, p. 157.
2   WorkSafeBC, *Occupational First Aid: A Reference and Training Manual*, p. 128.
3   ibid. p. 123.
4   ibid. p. 302.
5   Harvard School of Public Health, 'Alcohol: Balancing risks and benefits', online article in *The Nutrition Source*.
6   Mayo Clinic Staff, 'Alcohol: If you drink keep it moderate: Moderate alcohol use has possible health benefits, but it's not risk-free', online article 6 November 2018.
7   ibid.
8   World Health Organization (WHO). *Global Status Report on Alcohol and Health*, Box 9: Major disease and injury categories causally linked to alcohol', p. 22.

9 University of California, Berkeley, School of Public Health, 'Alcohol: What moderation means', online article in *Berkeley Wellness*, 7 March 2013.

10 ibid.

11 ibid.

12 American Heart Association (AHA), 'Alcohol and heart health', online article, updated 12 January 2015.

13 ibid.

14 ibid.

15 ibid.

16 ibid.

17 Mayo Clinic Staff, 'Alcohol: If you drink keep it moderate: Moderate alcohol use has possible health benefits, but it's not risk-free', online article 6 November 2018.

18 American Heart Association (AHA), 'Alcohol and heart health', online article, updated 12 January 2015.

19 Centre for Addiction and Mental Health (CAMH), *Alcohol and Chronic Health Problems*.

20 University of California, Berkeley, School of Public Health, 'Alcohol: What moderation means', online article in *Berkeley Wellness*, 7 March 2013.

21 Centre for Addiction and Mental Health (CAMH). 'Alcohol and chronic health problems', online article accessed February 2019.

22 Harvard School of Public Health, 'Alcohol: Balancing risks and benefits', online article in *The Nutrition Source*. .

23 ibid.

24 ibid.

25 ibid.

26 World Health Organization (WHO), 'Is harmful use of alcohol a public health problem?', online Q&A, updated May 2014.

27 University of California, Berkeley, School of Public Health, 'Alcohol: What moderation means', online article in *Berkeley Wellness*, 7 March 2013.

28 World Health Organization (WHO). *Global Status Report on Alcohol and Health,* Introduction, p. x.

29 ibid.

30 ibid. Box 9: 'Major disease and injury categories causally linked to alcohol', p. 22.

31 Anderson and Baumberg, *Alcohol in Europe: A Public Health Perspective,* Summary, p. 6.

32 World Health Organization (WHO). *Global Status Report on Alcohol and Health,* Introduction, p. xi.

33 HM Government, *The Government's Alcohol Strategy*, p. 21.
34 Bahá'u'lláh, *The Kitáb-i-Aqdas*, para. 155, p. 75.

3. The Temple of the Heart

1 Bahá'u'lláh, *Gleanings from the Writings of Bahá'u'lláh*, CIX, pp. 214–15.
2 Benson, Rasmussen and Zimmermann, *The Impact of Alcohol Control Policies on the Incidence of Violent Crime*, report submitted to the National Criminal Justice Reference Service – US Department of Justice, summary in *NIJ Journal*, no. 249 (July 2003), p. 30.
3 WHO, *Alcohol: Key facts*.
4 National Institute on Alcohol Abuse and Alcoholism, 'Economic costs of alcohol and drug abuse estimated at $246 Billion in the United States', news release, 13 May 1998.
5 World Bank, 'Gross Domestic Product 2015', in *World Development Indicators Database*.
6 ibid.
7 World Food Programme (WFP), 'Overview'.
8 WFP, 'Contributions to WFP in 2016'.
9 UNICEF, *Annual Report 2015*, p. 6.
10 ibid. p. 13.
11 WHO, *Programme Budget 2016–2017*, p. 2.
12 Jacobs, *NASA Acting Administrator Statement on Fiscal Year 2018 Budget Proposal*.
13 Anderson and Baumberg, *Alcohol in Europe: A Public Health Perspective*, p. 5.
14 Jernigan, *Global Status Report: Alcohol and Young People*, p. 7.
15 Canadian Centre on Substance Abuse, *Canadian Drug Summary*, p. 1.
16 ibid. pp. 6–7.
17 McCracken et al., *Evaluation of Alcohol Arrest Referral Pilot Schemes (Phase 2)*, Executive Summary, p. i.
18 HM Government, Home Office (United Kingdom), *The Government's Alcohol Strategy*, PM Foreword, p. 2.
19 ibid., Introduction, p. 3.
20 ibid. p. 9.
21 Anderson and Baumberg, *Alcohol in Europe: A Public Health Perspective*, p. 5.
22 ibid. p. 138.
23 Canadian Centre on Substance Abuse, *Proportions of Crimes Associated with Alcohol and Other Drugs in Canada*, p. 9.
24 ibid. p. 10.
25 Anderson and Baumberg, *Alcohol in Europe: A Public Health Perspective*, p. 140.

26 ibid. p. 198.
27 Bunge, Johnson and Baldé, *Exploring Crime Patterns in Canada*, p. 24.
28 ibid. p. 25.
29 WHO, *Alcohol and Injuries: Emergency Department Studies in an International Perspective*, p. iv.
30 ibid.
31 Bunge, Johnson and Baldé, *Exploring Crime Patterns in Canada*, p. 24.
32 Anderson and Baumberg, *Alcohol in Europe: A Public Health Perspective*, p. 139.
33 ibid. p. 196.
34 Jernigan, *Global Status Report: Alcohol and Young People*, p. 5.
35 US Department of Health and Human Services, *Substance Abuse Treatment and Domestic Violence,* p. 3.
36 WHO, *Alcohol: Key facts.*
37 ibid.
38 WHO, *Global Status Report on Alcohol and Health*, p. v.
39 ibid. p. 34.
40 Bahá'u'lláh, *Gleanings from the Writings of Bahá'u'lláh*, XLII, p. 93.
41 ibid. CXXX, p. 285.

4. The Temple of the Mind

1 'Abdu'l-Bahá, *Paris Talks*, no. 36, p. 114.
2 'Abdu'l-Bahá, *The Promulgation of Universal Peace*, p. 66.
3 ibid. p. 67.
4 ibid. pp. 67–8.
5 Abdu'l-Bahá, *Paris Talks*, no. 11, pp. 32, 34.
6 Bahá'u'lláh, *The Kitáb-i-Aqdas*, para. 119, p. 62.
7 Bahá'u'lláh, *Gleanings from the Writings of Bahá'u'lláh*, CLIII, p. 327.
8 'Abdu'l-Bahá, *Selections from the Writings of 'Abdu'l-Bahá*, no. 129, p. 149.
9 'Abdu'l-Bahá, *The Promulgation of Universal Peace*, p. 441.
10 ibid.
11 ibid.

5. The Temple of the Soul

1 Bahá'u'lláh, 'The Seven Valleys', in *The Call of the Divine Beloved*, p. 16.
2 'Abdu'l-Bahá, *Paris Talks*, no. 31, p. 96.

6. Ulysses and the Island of the Lotus-Eaters

1 Homer, *The Odyssey*, ed. Samuel Butler, Book IX.
2 ibid.

3 Bahá'í World Centre, *One Common Faith*, p. 47.
4 Herbert, *Chapterhouse: Dune*, section 38. p. 344.
5 On many Internet quotation sites.
6 Gupta (ed.), 'Katha Upanishad', ch. 2, vv. 1–2, in *Ethical Questions: East and West*, p. 49.
7 Bahá'u'lláh. *The Kitáb-i-Aqdas*, para. 125, pp. 63–4.

7. But What About the Weed?

1 Royal College of General Practitioners. 'Cannabis and the general practitioner – Going to Pot', section 'Possible therapeutic effects'.
2 Grinspoon, 'Medical marijuana'.
3 World Health Organization (WHO), *Cannabis: A Health Perspective and Research Agenda*, section 14: 'Therapeutic uses of cannabinoids', p. 30.
4 Centers for Disease Control and Prevention (CDC). 'Marijuana: How can it affect your health?', section 'Cancer'.
5 Note 170 in Bahá'u'lláh, *The Kitáb-i-Aqdas*, p. 239, referring to quotations from Tablets by 'Abdu'l-Bahá.
6 ibid.
7 Mayo Clinic, 'What are the benefits of CBD –and is it safe to use?'.
8 National Institute on Drug Abuse. 'Marijuana as medicine: What is medical marijuana?',
9 World Health Organization (WHO), *Cannabis: A Health Perspective and Research Agenda*, section 5.1: 'Acute effects on central nervous system functions and behaviour', p. 14.
10 ibid. section 5.2: 'Effects on driving', p. 15.
11 Centers for Disease Control and Prevention (CDC). 'Marijuana: How can it affect your health?', section 'Heart Health'.
12 ibid. section 'Lung health'.
13 ibid. section 'Cancer'.
14 Royal College of General Practitioners. 'Cannabis and the general practitioner – Going to Pot'.
15 ibid.
16 Hathaway, 'Study links genes to marijuana dependence and major depression', in *Yale News*, 30 March 2016.
17 Johns, 'Psychiatric effects of cannabis', in *The British Journal of Psychiatry*, vol. 178, no. 2 (Feb. 2001), pp. 119–20.
18 Ashton, 'Pharmacology and effects of cannabis: A brief review', ibid. pp. 101–106.
19 National Centre on Addiction and Substance Abuse (CASA), *Non-medical Marijuana: Rite of Passage or Russian Roulette?*, pp. 2–3.
20 Crean et al. 'An evidence based review of acute and long-term effects of

cannabis use on executive cognitive functions', in *Journal of Addiction Medicine*, vol. 5, no. 1 (2011), pp. 1–2.

21 Shrivastava et al. 'Cannabis use and cognitive dysfunction', in *Indian Journal of Psychiatry*, vol. 53, no. 3 (2011), section: 'Effect of cannabis on cognition'.

22 Ashton, 'Pharmacology and effects of cannabis: A brief review'.

23 ibid.

24 'Cannabis/Marijuana', online article in *Psychology Today*.

25 ibid.

26 ibid.

27 American Psychological Association, 'Regular marijuana use bad for teens' brains: Psychology and public health experts weigh in on potential effects of legalization on youth', press release 9 August 2014.

28 ibid.

29 Lisdahl et al., 'Considering cannabis: The effects of regular cannabis use on neurocognition in adolescents and young adults', in *Current Addiction Reports*, vol. 1, no. 2, p. 145.

30 Meier et al., 'Persistent cannabis users show neuropsychological decline from childhood to midlife', in *Proceedings of the National Academy of Sciences (PNAS)*. Published online 27 August 2012.

31 ibid.

32 National Centre on Addiction and Substance Abuse (CASA), *Nonmedical Marijuana: Rite of Passage or Russian Roulette?*, pp. 2–3.

33 Weir, 'Marijuana and the developing brain . . .', in *Monitor on Psychology*, vol. 46, no. 10 (Nov. 2015), p. 48.

34 Lisdahl et al., 'Considering cannabis: The effects of regular cannabis use on neurocognition in adolescents and young adults', in *Current Addiction Reports*, vol. 1, no. 2, p. 148.

35 National Institute on Drug Abuse (NIDA), *Is There a Link Between Marijuana Use and Psychiatric Disorders?*

36 ibid.

37 Canadian Centre on Substance Use and Addiction, '*Clearing the Smoke on Cannabis: Highlights – An update*'.

38 Royal College of Psychiatrists, Public Education Editorial Board, 'Cannabis'.

39 Harvard Medical School (Harvard Health Publications), 'Marijuana use may be harmful to mental health: The Family Health Guide', online article May 2003.

40 ibid.

41 ibid.

42 ibid.

43 ibid.

NOTES AND REFERENCES

8. Warriors of Light

1 'Abdu'l-Bahá, *Paris Talks*, no. 28, p. 83.
2 Bahá'u'lláh, *Epistle to the Son of the Wolf*, p. 55.
3 Bahá'u'lláh, Lawḥ-i-Hikmat, in *Tablets of Bahá'u'lláh Revealed After the Kitáb-i-Aqdas*, p. 139.
4 'Abdu'l-Bahá. *Selections from the Writings of 'Abdu'l-Bahá*, no. 208, pp. 276–7.
5 ibid. no. 207, pp. 272–3.
6 Letter from Shoghi Effendi to the American Baháʼí Community, 19 July 1956, in Shoghi Effendi, *Citadel of Faith*, pp. 148–9.
7 Abdu'l-Bahá. *Selections from the Writings of Abdu'l-Bahá*, no. 206, p. 256.
8 'Abdu'l-Bahá, cited in Shoghi Effendi, *The Advent of Divine Justice*, para. 40, p. 26.
9 Bahá'u'lláh, *Hidden Words*, Arabic no. 40.
10 Letter written on behalf of Shoghi Effendi to the National Spiritual Assembly of India, 30 June 1952, in Shoghi Effendi, *Dawn of a New Day*, p. 153; also in *Lights of Guidance*, no. 339, pp. 98–9.

9. The Homecoming Clean

1 'Abdu'l-Bahá, *Paris Talks*, no. 35, p. 110.
2 Letter from the Universal House of Justice to an individual, 3 January 1982, in *Messages from the Universal House of Justice 1963–1986*, no. 308, p. 517.

About the Author

Rob Cacchioni grew up in a small Canadian town, enmeshed in his own 'chemical pastimes' on the *'other side of the tracks'*. In his early 20s he moved to Vancouver to study counselling and personal coaching. Already a student of comparative religion, he there encountered the Bahá'ís. He investigated Bahá'u'lláh's claim and embraced His global vision. He spent several years in South Korea, Taiwan and Yemen. He now lives in Vancouver with his wife and two children, where he teaches martial arts and music, and regularly offers talks on religious unity. For 20 years, he's studied religion and philosophy and currently runs a YouTube channel called *Bridging Beliefs*, offering *bridges* between Bahá'u'lláh's vision and Christianity, Islam, Hinduism, Buddhism, Judaism, secularism and atheism.

www.ingramcontent.com/pod-product-compliance
Lightning Source LLC
Chambersburg PA
CBHW020906100426
42737CB00044B/390